I0458559

A Christian Theory of
Political Truth

A Christian Theory of Political Truth

Groen van Prinsterer

Translated by: Jan Adriaan Schlebusch

RefCon Press

A Christian Theory of Political Truth

Copyright © 2024

Published by **RefCon Press**
   7901 4ᵗʰ St. North Ste. #8193
   St. Petersburg, FL 33702

RefCon Press is the publishing imprint of:
The Reformed Conservative
www.thereformedconservative.org
admin@thereformedconservative.org

All rights reserved. No part of this publication may be reproduced, stored in a retrieval system, or transmitted in any form or by any means—electronic, mechanical, photocopy, recording, or any other—except for brief quotations in printed reviews, without the prior permission of the publisher.

Originally published in Dutch by Guillaume Groen van Prinsterer as *Proeve over de middelen waardoor de warheid wordt Gekend en Gestaafd*, first edition by Luchtmans (Leiden) in 1834; second edition by H. Höveker (Amsterdam) in 1858. This is a translation of the second edition, which is in the public domain.

All Scripture quotations are from The Holy Bible, The New King James Version®. Copyright © 1982 by Thomas Nelson. Used by permission. All rights reserved.

Library of Congress Control Number: 2024949753

ISBN: 978-1-954504-04-2 (Hardcopy)
ISBN: 978-1-954504-05-9 (eBook)

Translator: Jan Adriaan Schlebusch
General Editor: Robert J. McPherson II
Copy Editor: Elizabeth Sain
Cover Design: Onur Burconur

To the Reformed Conservatives
Defend. Strengthen. Build.

Contents

Translator's Preface ix

Preface to the Second Edition (1858) xiii

Preface to the First Edition (1834) xv

Editor's Introduction xxi

Introduction...xxvii

1. Principles.. 29

2. Revelation 47

    Christianity.. 48

    Protestantism 53

    Mysticism 68

3. Philosophy.. 71

4. History 83

    Part 1: Revelation and History 83

    Part 2: Philosophy and History....................... 101

5. General Agreement 117

Index 129

Translator's Preface

The first edition of this spectacular contribution on political epistemology by Guillaume Groen van Prinsterer (1801–1876) was originally published in 1834, fairly early in the Dutch anti-revolutionary statesman's life. Groen, as he is affectionately known, vehemently opposed the anti-Christian liberalism produced by the Enlightenment. Given that the central message of his numerous writings can best be summarized by saying that the forsaking of the supremacy of God's transcendent moral order in favor of the supremacy of mankind leads to arbitrary authority and consequently tyranny, it is impossible to thoroughly understand Groen's Christian-historical or anti-revolutionary political positions and engagement apart from his theory of political truth, his political epistemology. Groen dedicated his entire life to polemics against the French Revolution and the nineteenth-century European revolutions of his own time because he saw them as the sociopolitical manifestations of an epistemological revolution—a rebellion against the authority of the Triune God as revealed in the Bible. In light of this, it is rather surprising how little attention scholars have paid to his political theory. In fact, in overlooking this aspect of his thought, many scholars have wrongly interpreted Groen's anti-revolutionary position as entailing an opposition to political resistance (or "revolution") against tyranny as such, which in reality is the exact opposite of what he advocated. I hope that this translation, which presents Groen's most philosophical work to a broader international audience for the first time, will go a long way toward rectifying that mistake.

The original Dutch title of this work would, literally translated, read *Views on Politics and International Law, Part I: The Means by Which Truth Can Be Known and Confirmed.* In other words, it is quite literally a work dedicated to a Christian theory of political truth: investigating how we can distinguish truth from falsehood, and how this shapes our political epistemology.

As the second part of his envisaged series was never published, I have opted for a concise yet rather descriptive title for this first translation of the work into English: *A Christian Theory of Political Truth.*

In this book, Groen outlines the epistemic basis of his political theory, and in doing so he shows how the sovereign truths of divine revelation are manifested firstly in the Bible as God's Word, but then also through Providence in history, through philosophy as the pursuit of divine wisdom, and through the general agreement of all the generations through all ages, places, and times as participants in a single, unified created reality ordained and governed by God.

Groen published a second edition of this work much later in his career, which included a few minor additions via footnotes. I have included both of Groen's prefaces to the respective editions in this translation and used the text of the second edition as the basis of this translation, as it reflects the views of a more mature Groen. All Groen's footnotes are clearly indicated and italicized in order to distinguish them from my own annotation. Where Scripture is quoted, I have not simply translated the original Dutch from the *Statenvertaling* that Groen used, instead I used the text of the New King James version of the English Bible.

When I completed my PhD on Groen van Prinsterer between 2013 and 2018 at the University of Groningen in the Netherlands, this particular work proved most insightful in terms of understanding his phenomenal contribution to Christian political theory. It is my sincere hope that this translation will prove equally insightful to the readers thereof.

Jan Adriaan Schlebusch

Preface to the Second Edition
(1858)

This work initially saw the light of day in 1834, published as the first part of my envisioned series on *Views on Politics and International Law*. It constitutes an independent whole, however. Here I provide the readers with a reprint, not a revision. I have added a few short comments here and there that were not included in the first edition. Quotations that we now generally regard as irrelevant have also been omitted. In a few instances it will still be important to remember that this text was initially published in the early 1830s. Since that time, my convictions have not merely remained constant but have in fact been strengthened by what I have learned from both books and experiences since the publication of the first edition. A work on the means by which truth can be known and confirmed will always remain relevant, but perhaps more so now than ever, given the woeful condition of the fatherland brought about by the episodes of the past few decades. One of my friends, who is most knowledgeable regarding the spirit of our age, accurately described the current condition in

January of this year as "moral exhaustion and a commonly held doubt regarding the possibility of any Christian principles again having an impact on society, along with the constant humiliation of all who advocate these Christian principles." This is how the year 1858 has been in the Netherlands, and that is the reality of this discouraging sentiment. Therefore, a repetition of the praise of the truth of the gospel that characterized this work in 1834 is now, twenty-four years later, just as necessary as it has ever been. It will be seen that this effort to show that the foundation and the standard of all knowledge lies not only in history but above all in that which has been revealed is by no means redundant.

The Hague, December 1858

Preface to the First Edition
(1834)

Circumstances, the nature of which cannot be discussed here, have drawn me away from a highly regarded position to the desirable seclusion of a more homely life. The rest that I am hereby afforded cannot pass by idly at my young age and I certainly cannot afford not to spend my free time productively. I am in the position where I can spend my energy as I desire, but it cannot be spent only for myself. Therefore, I will attempt to fulfill my duties as a Christian and a Dutchman, since my one talent must be employed to the benefit of others. This conviction has brought me to realize the need to publish the fruits of my labor in this first volume on my views on politics and international law.

With this publication I hope to please those who became dissatisfied after I sorrowfully ceased publication of the magazine, *Dutch Ideas*.[1] After all, the

---

[1] Groen published his own magazine entitled *Dutch Ideas* (*Nederlandse Gedachten*) between 1830 and 1832, following his realization of the importance of journalism in promoting his anti-revolutionary convictions. After retiring from his

work which I now present to my fellow countrymen, albeit very different in nature, can be seen as a modified continuation of my previous work. It is written for the same purpose: to revive the Christian faith, patriotism, the dutiful submission to legitimate authority, and the rightful appreciation of the true liberty that alone is reconcilable with true authority. It is based on the same foundations—revealed truth and historical reality. I would have preferred to call this work "Christian-Historical Views," but I regard it as redundant to mention that which in the treatment of the subject will speak for itself, and I regard it as almost inadequate to give my own label to that which I regard to be the condition, yes the *conditio sine qua non*, of all truth, rights, and morality.

The ideas that have guided my thinking shall be made evident in this first part, which will probably not be followed up by a second part for quite some time.[2] An outline in which I carefully lay out the foundation from which I proceed to the sphere of politics and international law seems unmissable at a time characterized by so many controversies and when I am obliged to take sides on so many issues.[3] Writing this

---

career as a statesman four decades later, he would again continue publishing new editions of this magazine throughout the early 1870s—the final years of his life.

[2] *Groen: A second part, as I had intended here, will never be published.*

[3] Here Groen probably has the *Afscheiding* (Separation) of 1834 in mind, which had taken place in that same year. With this church division, the conservatives, also known as the *Afgescheidenen*, split from the national Dutch Reformed Church because of the rise of theological liberalism in that denomination. Groen sympathized with the theological orthodoxy of the *Afgescheidenen* yet chose to remain within the structures of the national church. He regarded the National Reformed Church as an integral part and treasure

work was no easy or unemotional task, and I have entitled this outline on the means by which truth is known and confirmed an "essay" for the sake of precaution: meaning that I sincerely confess my mistrust in my own human strength and that I am willing to subject the results of my study to the test of a better judgment and a more perfect knowledge.

The reader must judge the appropriateness of the numerous short comments and notes contained in this work. The deliberate extension of notes, and the multiplication and the agglomeration of citations, which people often call "learned citations," is an art I have never regarded particularly highly. Unless of course you, the reader, demand that I add clumsiness on top of my limited knowledge. I would argue that I actually quote sparingly, for if you consider that someone like me, who opposes the dominant ideas of this age, cannot expect much support, you would see that I have to take extra care to appeal to the witness of competent judges in order to validate my conviction that my argument is pure and to make any inroads. Yes, I ought not to take even one step forward without having shown that I am firmly rooted on the solid ground of proven and commonly held truths. My notes could have been added as endnotes rather than footnotes, but endnotes are only suitable for the type of comments that are only indirectly related to the text. And these are exactly the type of comments I have sought to avoid. Endnotes are not often read anyway, except by those who are not deterred by constantly having to look up references—and it is certainly not my intention not to accommodate a broader reading public for their sake. Also, the reading of the text need not be

---

of Dutch nationhood, especially as a national moral compass for both the people and the government.

interrupted by notes. In fact, I would prefer it if the reader read the text twice: first without and thereafter with the notes. But it may be that this wish of mine, especially in our day characterized by short and brief literature, will remain unfulfilled. Yet, on the other hand, what profit is there in scanning a work of which the contents will only benefit the attentive reader.

I am aware that the unabashed expression of my sentiments can lead to readers' experiences that may seem unsatisfactory. Those who are more inclined to seek their own benefit than the truth do not currently write on these kinds of controversial topics but instead, in order to remain safe within the confines of public opinion, only publish the kind of works we commonly call popular works. Self-sacrifice and bravery are needed in order to have the confidence to engage in endeavors such as these. I hope that I am not being immodest when I claim these virtues for myself. On the contrary, I think I am actually often wrongly inclined to forget that the truth itself has rights—the greatest rights—and that love actually becomes lovelessness when it seeks peace and agreement over the truth, especially when the desire for peace, combined with an indifference toward orthodoxy, becomes indolence and sacrilege. Also, it is important to remember that it is never permissible to spare evil simply for the sake of protecting people's feelings. Therefore, the seriousness and intensity of any expression must correlate with the topic at hand, and it would be immoral to not boldly proclaim the whole truth for the sake of satisfying the reader.

If I have therefore not violated the laws of modesty, I believe I have the right to request certain concessions from the reader in return. The reader must keep in mind that I am publishing this work as an introduction to works I intend to publish at a later stage, even if it consists of an independent whole in itself. An introduction, yes—but oh, as boundless as our human intentions, so limited are our actual achievements. The brevity of the years of human life, described as "soon cut off, and we fly away" (Psalm 90:10), should not discourage but rather encourage us. It reminds us that the correct application of true knowledge is of greater importance than the mere accumulation thereof. How many scholars are guilty of simply accumulating for the sake of building up a reputation without fulfilling their duty of sharing and correctly applying this knowledge? God addresses them when He says: "Fool! This night your soul will be required of you; then where will those things be which you have provided?" (Luke 12:20). The *memento mori* must be written at the entrance of the study especially, to remind each and every scholar of his mortality, so that we can use the time allotted to us to the best of our abilities and not have any regrets at the hour of our death. While appreciating the praise of men, we ought to regard the judgment of the Lord above all, in order that we may, by God's grace, know Christ as our Lord and Redeemer. We must not sacrifice that which is of eternal value for the sake of a false wisdom. Life itself, as the old philosophers taught, ought to be a gradual contemplation of the reality of death. But only when this contemplation becomes a truly Christian preparation for death, or let us rather say eternal life, does human action acquire true direction and purpose in accordance with the chief end of our existence.

The Hague, July 1, 1834

Editor's Introduction

You hold in your hands the answer to the political problem of our time. Actually, I must make a correction. You hold half the answer. The other half is titled *Liberty, Equality, Fraternity: A Refutation of Liberalism*. These two works were never intended to be published together. But, in truth, they are two sides to the same coin. Both are necessary for a full-orbed picture. Both address the supreme political problem of our time from a theological vantage point. And since an introduction is meant to help the reader best prepare himself to understand what he is about to read, I would be remiss if I did not point you to Groen's earlier work. It may not help the first read, but surely may help future rereads.

In short, what is the problem and what is the solution as Groen sees it? The problem is politics which have gone awry due to being devoid of sound political and ethical principles, a problem that is the result of a social and political rejection of the living God. This is a sentiment that Christian conservatives today fully agree with.

It's worth emphasizing at the expense of both stating the obvious and being overly redundant that Groen's take is decidedly and unapologetically both conservative and Christian. Naturally, these two go hand in hand, as it were. In order of importance and reliability, Groen argues that political principles are, or ought to be, founded upon revelation, philosophy, history, and the general agreement of all people at all times. These are the four sources of truth, not all truth, but political truth. If a Christian statesman is looking for guidance, he has but to turn to these four sources to guide him. Such a method would set a man at direct odds with the Enlightenment, and thus liberal political methods. For liberal politics has, historically, rejected revelation as superstitious, in favor of "neutral" means; rejected history and general agreement as morally arbitrary; and has rejected sound philosophy for, as Groen contends, any philosophy disconnected from sound theology will certainly go astray. What follows in this introduction is an explanation of each chapter.

Groen opens his book with a chapter on the nature of first principles themselves, arguing that the current lack of principles in the political and social spheres is due to apostasy from God. When God and His Word are not seen as the ultimate source of truth, then all truth is reduced to prejudice and ignorance. Consequently, the supremacy of individual reason becomes the guiding principle, a rationalism where each man does what is right in his own eyes. This leads to the forsaking of true ethical and political principles and the overthrow of solid ideas and godly institutions, especially in politics. And this has been nowhere more evident than the French Revolution and its aftermath, where the quest for liberty and equality led to tyranny and oppression. Groen concludes that the only way to restore true principles in the life of a nation is to return to God as the source of all truth.

In the second chapter, Groen explores the importance of Divine Revelation as a source of political truth, directly addressing the Protestant Reformation, defining it as nothing less than true Christianity. Christianity is the foundation for all political and moral truth. The Reformation aimed to return to the original principles of the apostolic and orthodox catholic faith. It must be understood that neither the Roman Catholic Church nor rationalist and liberal theologies are a reliable source of truth, let alone political truth, due to their unchristian doctrines and practices. Mysticism is also a misleading source of political truth, for it distorts the harmony between mind and heart, leading to either a rationalist reaction or a sentimentalist religion. He concludes by advocating for a political theory that aligns with Christian truth.

In the third chapter, the great Dutch parliamentarian and historian argues that true philosophy is inseparable from true religion, and that Christianity is the only true religion. Defective religious principles always lead to defective philosophy; only Christianity can be the foundation of true philosophy. And if this is true of philosophy in general, it is true of political philosophy in particular.

Groen asserts that the relationship between religion and philosophy has always been acknowledged, and that the highest philosophy is the knowledge of God. Unbelief has caused an unnatural separation between Christianity and philosophy. In contending that all philosophical systems apart from Christian philosophy are flawed and false, Groen even took aim at our Greco-Roman heritage. Greek philosophy, despite its merits, lacks clarity, purity, completeness, and certainty, yet Christianity offers an explanation and purification of such pagan philosophy.

Regarding the fourth chapter, Groen starts with a general critique of secular history, arguing that Christ's redemptive work is at its very center, thus the non-Christian view of history is unsatisfactory. Even the pagans of antiquity were aware of divine influence on the world, although they had many misconceptions. Today, due to the Enlightenment, apostasy from Christianity has shaped the dominant view of history which forsakes the notion of a personal God and rejects history's religious character. A deistic view of history is distorted. God and the Christian faith—a historical faith—play a vital role in both the discipline of history and the national life of a people. Without true religion, civilization would nearly cease. So too, without a solid foundation in history, political theory becomes just as deranged and moribund.

Perhaps Groen's most important point in this chapter is the relationship between political theory and history, that is, the nature of false political theories that are so "pure" that they reject history. True political philosophy investigates the nature of things and history contains the mold, the imprint, as it were, of that nature. A false political theory, by contrast, proceeds from arbitrary ideas and presuppositions. The Enlightenment produced many false and arbitrary political theories that are anti-historical and anti-national. The true political theory is simple: "maintain and improve," not "destroy and recreate."

The astute reader will recognize the fact that communists and socialists continue to ignore the consistent failures of their respective systems in history, since they divorce theory from it, the very issue Groen takes aim at. Due to rejecting the validity of historical insight, the unbeliever has no foundation for a solid understanding of law and state. This mistake is like a biologist or psychologist not describing people as they are but only as he expects them to be. But if political theory can neither be proven nor disproven by history, then only arbitrary tyranny will reign in the realm of political ideas. As a fruit of this unbelief, a system of perfectibility is common among false political ideas, yet the Christian should know that there is no utopia this side of heaven.

In the fifth and final chapter, Groen discusses the value of general agreement, public opinion, and the judgment of competent judges. General agreement consists of the truths that all people have agreed on throughout the ages. The value of this agreement is significant, and truth can often be found within it, since universality is a characteristic of truth, although not the cause or foundation of it. Nevertheless, public opinion is different from general agreement, being more susceptible to the influence of self-interest and emotions. Furthermore, public sentiment is often formed prematurely and is not a reliable standard. That notwithstanding, he acknowledges that public opinion can be shaped and controlled through the natural power of principles and that the judgment of competent judges, or experts, should be valued. However, in the current age, expertise is often falsely claimed. Groen concludes that general agreement should be valued more than public opinion, and that true principles should always guide one's judgment.

The reader is owed one final explanation: why another introduction on top of the original author's introduction? The short answer is for the sake of following many modern introductions which provide said introduction by way of summary. An introduction is meant to help the reader get the most out of the reading. It is this editor's opinion that that more was needed to make the most of the opportunity, especially in our own day when the ability to read has been degraded so significantly. In our cultural and political climate, too much is at stake. It is imperative that Christian conservatives proclaim the truth with all the clarity and boldness they can muster.

BJM
General Editor

Introduction

A ll science necessarily and inescapably has its first principles. Regardless of the subject under investigation, at the start of research, there are certain accepted truths upon which the study itself is dependent. These truths ensure the stability of the scientific building and without these truths, the results of such investigations can only be delusions. So it is with all science, so it is with law. All research and presentation is in vain when it is not founded upon solid ground.

Yet there exists a dispute over these first principles. What one acknowledges as such, the other does not. What one regards as a sure and true foundation, the other regards as either false or dubious. Each man argues in accordance with his principles, or rather, in accordance with what he regards to be first principles. Therefore it would be helpful if, prior to any other arguments, it is investigated whether opposing parties could achieve more agreement with regard to these core principles.[4]

---

[4] Groen immediately begins his discussion of epistemology with a reference to the presuppositions that shape the

Everything must be tested against these higher truths in which the foundations of each and every science are rooted. But even this is not enough. These general truths themselves, by which alone unanimity can be achieved, are currently widely doubted and scrutinized and as a result everything, including national and international law, have become wobbly.

Mankind has not been left to itself—God has revealed Himself in 1) Holy Scripture, therein lies the highest truth and therein we have an undeceiving standard; 2) reason as the tool of philosophy; 3) history, through which the life and outworking of principles become visible; and 4) general agreement that points to these truths, even if it does not prove them.

---

theoretical framework from which human beings interpret the realities around us. This view would later famously be echoed by Gordon Clark, who wrote that: "Every philosophic or theological system must begin somewhere, for if it did not begin it would not continue. But a beginning cannot be preceded by anything else, or it would not be a beginning. Therefore every system must be based on presuppositions (required as a precondition of possibility and coherence, tacitly assumed to be the case) or axioms (an accepted statement or proposition regarded as being self-evidently true). They may be Spinoza's axioms; they may be Locke's sensory starting point, or whatever. Every system must therefore be presuppositional. The first principle cannot be demonstrated because there is nothing prior from which to deduce it" (Gordon Clark, *A Christian Philosophy of Education* [Grand Rapids, MI: Eerdmans, 1946], 41).

1
Principles

What are principles? From where does the general lack of principles characteristic of our time come? How can this licentiousness be curbed and brought to an end? Answering these questions will reveal how people are led to God through principles, and how apostasy has brought about this unscrupulousness, and finally that steadfast principles can be regained solely by acknowledging God's authoritative revelation.

What are principles? Principles are accepted truths by which every investigation is enabled—that is, acknowledged truths that form the foundation of every argument. These truths can often in themselves be conclusions derived from higher truths. In this way we can climb up from high principles to even higher principles, until we acquire the highest truths, which are indubitable and not subject to scrutiny—objects of faith, which are the starting point of any science. These are the principles that are rooted in God's will and nature par excellence.

From these first principles, all that are commonly called "principles" in the sciences are to be derived.

Propositions that are initially subject to doubt and that need to be proven, are proven with the aid of these highest principles and thus are sufficiently substantiated in order to reach a state of undeniability and certainty. In this way, the seal of being undoubted is impressed upon any research. And it is by means of this continual formation of secondary principles, which transition from being dubitable to being undoubtedly sure, that science progresses. But it is always unto God that the whole chain of human knowledge is bound up. Therefore, the question regarding the current general lack of principles is not difficult to answer.

Apostasy from God is the cause thereof.[5] The history of the past few decades would need to be erased from books and from memory in order to deny the apostasy of this age as well as the fact that atheism has been promoted as the first principle of the sciences. The decline of the Christian Church and the forsaking of morals have paved the way for theoretical unbelief.[6] Thereby the philosophy of the eighteenth century was able to make its appearance: God and His Word were

---

[5] *Groen: The new philosophy calls indubitable that which is based in uncertainty. It has also reduced principles to opinions and certainty to doubt.*

[6] This is the core of Groen's anti-revolutionary theory. At the heart of his theo-political position lies the conviction that the Enlightenment of the eighteenth century affected sociopolitical and scientific decline, and that any progress made during the first few decades of the nineteenth century came in spite of and not because of the Enlightenment. In his book, *How the Catholic Church Built Western Civilization*, Tom Woods offers a valuable critique of the narrative that it was the Enlightenment that brought about the Industrial Revolution by pointing out that it was monks in monasteries who had built furnaces to extract iron from ore, which served as prototypes to usher in the industrial age (Thomas E. Woods, Jr., *How the Catholic Church Built Western Civilization* [Washington, DC: Regnery, 2005], 37).

not regarded to be the source and standard of truth anymore but rather man and his reason. Since then, the sciences have declined, and since theory is never without any impact in practice, the resultant fall of states has also become inevitable. Denying God and idolizing oneself always leads to the forsaking of true principles and the overthrow of (solid) ideas and institutions. A revolutionary period had to follow— whereby people were led to forsake and become indifferent toward principles. This could have been easily predicted—it was, in fact, predicted—and the reason for this societal decline cannot be sought elsewhere.

As soon as the source and essence of all truth is not acknowledged, all truth is reduced to prejudice and ignorance. The apostate philosophers reduce all faith to superstition. They claim that our ancestors walked in darkness, were headed in the wrong direction, and built upon deceptive foundations. Their common heritage, which they regard as valuable as gold, is merely a worthless coin as they have no solid standard. And so the supremacy of individual reason, the principle without principles, seeks to overthrow all that religion and science have historically achieved. Destruction was their common desire—and it was no difficult task. But thereafter something had to be put in the place of faith. But what? Regarding this question, a thousand answers came up, but there was no general agreement. The principles themselves were powerless, so it is no wonder that such a chaotic mixture of opinions arose. In the midst of this confusion, there was a desire for something certain and unshakable, and since no higher source of knowledge was recognized, this certainty was sought in human speculation. System upon system was developed and the masses were constantly swept along by the apparent genius of some influential figure until finally, in their revolt against the supremacy of true principles, they bowed like slaves before every vain and empty theory. System upon system again sunk away into the darkness. By means of false theories, the people developed an aversion to theory itself. So often the truth was promised only to deliver nothing, and what has, the people cynically ask, that vain search and all those attempts achieved? "What is truth? Does truth exist? Oh, truth is an idle promise," people say.

These same developments can be seen especially in the field of politics. States are being demolished. Liberation from religion means liberation from legitimate authority. Humanity, seen as the source of truth, has become its own lawgiver—granting permission to ourselves has come to be regarded as the shaky foundation of obedience and duty.[7] But this theory quickly led to an unprecedented disaster. Now the neo-propositional state would be founded. But how? This is a difficult question and one that they only achieved in answering by means of armed responses. The unification of philosophical liberty with social order was attempted in various ways—differing forms of government and political systems alternated with each other—but the end was always tyranny and suppression.[8] Groaning under tyranny, people longed

---

[7] Groen argues that without a supreme, divine Lawgiver and His moral standard, mankind devolves into complete anarchy and licentiousness. Within his historical context, Groen was convinced that European civilization stood before an inevitable and inescapable choice: either submit to the authority of God and His revelation or reject it and experience detrimental decline as a result.

[8] Groen would later elucidate this claim in Lectures XI–XIV of his magnum opus, *Unbelief and Revolution*, wherein he provides a historical outline of the development of the Revolution, which he then also utilizes as an appeal to fellow

for liberty and believed that if only the government could be exchanged for another, the supremacy of the people could finally be achieved. But eventually they became disillusioned after a series of disappointments. Despite so many governments coming to a fall, the despotism continued, and how then can the search for liberty continue? Liberty, they sigh, is not a reality, but a dream that perpetually remains at a distance, and the moment people believe they have achieved it, it flies away again.[9]

Now we see despair everywhere and consequently indifference to principles, contentment with the opinion of the day, passive submission to that which people like to call the order of the day, and an obsession with material matters to the extent that those things which belong to higher spheres are either disregarded or completely sacrificed. This is what systematic unbelief, if allowed to continue unchecked, eventually effectuates. And these are, in fact, the characteristics of the apostasy of our age.

And what lamentable characteristics these are! Delighting in a false doctrine also produces zeal and diligence, and these energies only need to be redirected to truth in order to produce the most glorious fruits. But indifference is fatal for the soul and all that is good and noble is destroyed by it. Because of indifference,

---

Christians to take action to advance the kingdom of God— also in the public domain.

[9] *Groen: The current condition of religion, morality, and science is the fruit by which the tree of unbelief can be known. The history of Europe, after anti-Christian ideas took hold and a series of revolutions unfolded, does not consist of anything but that which is the inevitable result of revolutionary politics. The overview of this history can be found in my* Nederlandsche Gedachten. *It is important to remember the atheistic-philosophical origins of the European revolutions, especially those in France.*

people are dragged into the deepest pits of depravity where they play with principles as a child plays with toys. You might wonder if my judgment is not too harsh and if I am not exaggerating–especially with regard to the condition in the Netherlands. Well, there is indeed much that is praiseworthy in our time. Christianity has not been destroyed and wherever it remains, it still is, as it has always been, a blessing to the people— especially now as it is reviving and gaining renewed strength in many places. In such cases, evil is subdued, and these exceptions must be acknowledged as is always the case when one analyzes the spirit of the age, but this certainly does not in any way negate the prevalent characteristics of our time.

In politics and international relations, this indifference is striking. Even if there are those who continue to fight tooth and nail for false doctrines, they now make up a minority.[10] Previously they desired liberty at the cost of peace, but now they prefer peace, even if there is no liberty. The revolutionaries might claim liberty, truth, and right, but as soon as the interests of the state or the circumstances shamelessly demand its annulment, it is trampled upon. Even in terms of international law and international relations, maintaining the status quo has become the highest good, and even the so-called inalienable rights are subjected hereunto. Whereas they previously regarded justice as something to be maintained even at the cost of peace, they currently seek to maintain peace to such an extent that justice does not even come into

---

[10] *Groen: The kind of fanaticism that, when misled by false theories, values convictions over personal interest, was common during the first French Revolution of 1789 but not during the second French Revolution of 1830. Currently, the zealous ultraliberals and fanatical republicans in France are certainly a minority.*

consideration. Yet they do not always forsake principles. In fact, they fervently preach them and carry them along wherever they may be useful, but hypocrisy is committed with the truth, and in the name of the interest of Europe, they currently betray that which they had previously propagated.

This characteristic spirit of the age is especially revealed in France. This we must realize, not to comfort ourselves when we compare her to our own country, but to help notice whatever has been clearly revealed whenever it emerges elsewhere—even if it is veiled under deceptive forms. There in France, the unbelief has been transferred from the higher classes to the whole society. It has mastered most of the middle and lower classes as well. It teaches that there is no God and no eternal life—or at least not one that concerns us. Materialism is the order of the day.[11] The literature reveals the zeitgeist. Most of the productions of the past few years are characterized by the absence of any truth and virtue. It is not necessary to read a great deal of this literature to realize that good and evil are considered to be one and the same and that the distinction between morality and immorality becomes completely blurred. Faith is completely discarded, nothing is honored, everything is desecrated, and every remnant of zeal is banned.[12]

---

[11] *Groen: Unbelief was, with the first French Revolution, yet to be established as a truly national religion. The remnants of true religion among the lower classes had, in the midst of all the tyranny, helped to limit that tyranny. But eventually, unbelief became common among them as well.*

[12] The desecration of that which is in reality beautiful according to God's design has always been characteristic of the revolutionary agenda. R. J. Rushdoony, in his book *To Be as God: A Study of Modern Thought Since the Marquis de Sade,* highlighted the continuing role of subversion, and especially sexual subversion, inherent to the liberal and

These consequences of the prevailing theories of our time are not limited to France. These same teachings have had a similar impact elsewhere. However, by virtue of the lively French spirit and character,[13] they have been more thoroughly developed and applied there. Yet unbelief has also been succeeded by indifference in other countries. A complete lack of character and integrity has become more common than it has ever been before and the public actions and our time produces almost nothing that is not thoroughly petty.

Praising one's own country is flattering. This panegyrist can find many sympathetic ears and he himself shares in the praise he directs at his countrymen. But a people must also be heedful against self-elevation and deception. "Know thyself" is not only an important lesson applicable to individuals but this reproach regarding pride, haughtiness, and lovelessness, I must admit, is applicable to the Netherlands as well.

The Dutch have achieved much. We have an honorable place in the scene of European history. Yet this greatness, intrinsically related to our Christian national life, passed as soon as apostasy set in. What gain is there to glory in the achievements of ancestors if the progeny only remember them for the sake of further encouraging pride and egomania? Indolence, comfort, and self-interest currently dictate our national life. Here, too, the soil has been prepared for the implanting of revolutionary theories. The immoral

---

Marxist agenda (R. J. Rushdoony, *To Be as God: A Study of Modern Thought Since the Marquis de Sade* [Vallecito, CA: Ross House, 2003]).

[13] It is noteworthy that Groen recognizes the reality that every nation has its unique national spirit and character, along with its unique strengths and weaknesses.

and godless writings, multiplied by our printing presses, are well-received among many of our countrymen. The seed develops in the fruit that results in the hybridization of the ancestral character, the diminishing of the Christian faith, conflict, the upheaval of the state, and the replacement of every revolutionary government with another that is merely different in shape and form but not in essence. The support for our revolution can be found in France, but it took on a distinctly Dutch character as well. And what were the results? God delivered us from French occupation, but were we thereafter less influenced by the prevailing theories? For during the decades since our independence we have remained enchanted by the revolutionary propaganda, and our judgments have been greatly determined by Parisian newspapers.[14] We rejoiced when the liberals praised our liberalism, and thereby we blindly continued our approach into that abyss that we are bound to fall and crash into.

Therefore, it is unlikely that the Netherlands will be spared from the further consequences of the revolutionary development, especially since indifference and stolidity are now cultivated in our national life and by our new national character.

Far be it from me to deny the outstanding characteristics of the Dutch nation, yet, sadly, the

---

[14] *Groen: You may claim that* Louis XVIII *(the king of France from 1814 to 1824) was a counterrevolutionary and* Charles X *(king of France from 1824 to 1830) was a despot, but I am convinced that they, by their rejection of and rage against the Jesuits, meant to include all Christianity, including us. They sought the salvation of the state in ministerial responsibility and a free press, and we echoed them. The illegal revolt, the July Revolution of 1830, has, as well in the Netherlands, been greeted as a victory for liberty and national rights. We ought to have been much more careful and wise in our judgments.*

Dutch are currently plagued by a distinct lukewarmness and a tardiness through which the foggy climate of the day is revealed. Why would one try to deny this? If cultivated by higher principles, our national temperament could be a source of sobriety and composure—the Dutch have, after all, achieved many great things that are incompatible with indifference, and it is doubly praiseworthy that in practicing our virtues we have not merely sought self-gain. But let us not ignore the danger in this undeniable characteristic. It can become a defect when the zeal to do good is extinguished thereby, and it can provide a pretense of virtue for that which is unworthy of the name. There is an abstention from evil, not because of aversion, but rather because evil would require too much exertion and resilience. In this regard we differ from others—not because our heart and principles are in the right place, but because we regard utter depravity as too much effort and too dangerous. We only go halfway because we do not have the heart to be consistent. This unique national spirit also applies to our economy. Holland lives by trade. Who would deny that herein lies the unmissable economic backbone of the fatherland? But this mercantile spirit inevitably tends toward greed and self-interest. If the merchant does manage to rise above this, he will not conquer the undesirable tendencies of enterprise—lamentable tendencies that have always been acknowledged.[15]

There is but one means by which the negative effects of enterprise on our nature can be defeated. Nations are composed of people, and it is the true

---

[15] *Groen: The ancient philosophers feared the consequences of trade. Plato believed an accumulation of money would lead to a decline in virtue. According to Cicero, "it is not only the reward that is important, but also the cultivation of morals."*

religion alone that can liberate man from slavery unto sin. The reason that the Netherlands has risen to such great heights and great glory despite these obstacles is the Christian faith.

This observation provides us with the standard by which we are to judge our present condition. While it is true that we have escaped the depraved influences to which other nations have succumbed, the assumption is that our adherence to the gospel must have remained strong. But let us not flatter ourselves. In the Netherlands, shaped by Christianity more so than any other country, much that is Christian has remained. Here we have also witnessed the return of many to biblical truths. Yet, even in the estimation of the most benevolent analysts, the condition of the Protestant Churches was, during the revolutionary period, unsuitable to successfully resist such a powerful heresy.

Let us not shy away from a closer investigation of our condition. How much, people question, can be attributed to our fortunate circumstances? We are separated from Belgium and liberated from French influence. Patriotism has revealed itself in our glorious deeds and is seen in our sense of truth and justice as well as our aversion to revolutionary doctrines.

The first advantage is one I also appreciate. To remain unified with Belgium in the way we were could not but lead to the perdition of all that is precious to the Netherlands.[16] However, regarding the rest of the

---

[16] Groen lived in Brussels when the Belgian Revolution broke out in 1830 and as such experienced it firsthand. For Groen, the Brussels he experienced in the late 1820s in the run-up to the Belgian Revolution represented a revolutionary spirit to which he would dedicate his life to fighting. He rejected it as an anti-Christian spirit of anarchy and destruction with no vision beyond satisfying immediate sinful human impulses.

so-called advantages, I have my doubts. The French influence, which has always been fatal to us, remains greater than many estimate it to be. Contemporary literature, while horrid, apparently remains readable to many. Much bravery has been shown, and I do have to give credit where credit is due, but one should not exaggerate this to an absurd degree, as is done by those who fail to see that our victories have been largely due to the cowardice of our enemies more so than to our own heroism. Those who see in the national self-interest only self-sacrifice and those who refuse to acknowledge the weaknesses of the Dutch people by focusing exclusively on our strengths are especially prone to this misinterpretation. And when people tend to boast nowadays, they completely disregard the principles of politics and international law. The Netherlands has indeed maintained its sovereignty, but in our international relationships we have in reality maintained very few true principles.[17] By virtue of

---

[17] *Groen: Neither liberal nor anti-liberal principles played any role in terms of balancing our self-interest. Would not many have enjoyed seeing the complete destruction of Poland by the Russians during the November uprising? Would not many have preferred to see those of both parties—those supporting the grand duke as well as those supporting the Polish Republicans—destroy each other? Was there any active support or even sympathy for the many people in France and elsewhere who dearly sought to maintain their legal monarchy? Were there any who cared for the fact that the conservative residents of Vendée in France and the Carlists of northern Spain were, because of their unfailing faithfulness, hunted in the forests and mountains as wild beasts by the revolutionaries? In other words, have we shown any love by standing up for justice where it did not concern our own national interest? Because of this selfishness, we are being judged. We would have actually taken better care of our national interests by also considering the interests of others.*

being constantly blown back and forth, people have become confused by the theories yet have shown no interest in true anti-revolutionary politics and have continued to ally themselves with the revolutionaries who arc currently not only conquering by the convulsions of anarchy but are also trampling on all legal rights and liberties.

The very idea of principles causes hesitancy and dismay among many. They desire to hear nothing more of it. These people would banish the truth because of the damage that lies have done. They argue that by taking away his life, the sufferer is healed. Thankfully, the return to the source of all truth is a better remedy.[18]

Let us now turn our attention to this better remedy. Unscrupulousness, caused by apostasy, will never stop unless God is again acknowledged as the source of truth. Once this acknowledgment has taken place, many good things that would have been rejected by unbelief will be restored to their proper places. The fog will be removed and that which many have considered to belong to the past will again be revealed. I do not advocate a return to some old notions, however, which have rightly been replaced by the superior insight of later ages. I speak of principles that are never subject to change.

---

[18] *Groen: I do not agree with those who argue for the good fruits of our current political system. The cause of our relative prosperity lies in our love for the House of Orange, in our respect for the king, and in the remnants of religiosity. But so little of it can be attributed to our constitutional government itself. I would gladly ask the Senate and the House of Representatives if they think my earlier predictions of them being forced to surrender both their influence and authority were exaggerated. The patriot should not glory in the current political system, which has caused us many sacrifices, both unlawful and preposterous.*

Let us not occupy ourselves with the forms of arbitrary systems. Our aversion thereof is completely justified. Any system must be based upon principles and true principles themselves are never the products of human ingenuity. But if God does not exist, it is said, then God has to have been imagined. What a vain delusion! A god of our imagination—a human creation—is without any power. Similarly, principles based upon human convention are of no use. It is like a mere portrait of the sun on the wall, which provides no heat, life, or fecundity. Yet, while rejecting these illusions, let us not forget the essence in which alone the true foundation lies. God exists even if people made from dust and ashes deny His existence. The sun does not cease to exist because people seek shelter from its basking rays. Likewise, principles have an independent existence and are in no way dependent upon their acknowledgment—an acknowledgment that they either do or do not enjoy.

For the sake of science itself, it is also important to return to God as He has revealed Himself, and Christianity must be made explicit in the practice of all the sciences. Nonetheless, the reality of our day is that even many Christians oppose this.

It should not surprise us that the Christian approach to the sciences is a stumbling block to non-Christians. It seems ridiculous to those who regard the Holy Bible as an aggregation of frivolous myths, or as a purely historical document mixed with Middle Eastern mythology, and Christianity itself as merely one of many forms of expressing the religious desire to venerate a supreme being. And no wonder: philosophy has always sought to rid itself from what it regards as embarrassing and prohibitive superstition. Plato did not base his doctrine of ideas upon Greek misconceptions. The high personalities in Rome to which the oversight of divination was entrusted could barely contain their laughter and mockery. Before the Reformation it was even granted to high-ranking church officials to be Roman Catholics in the church but free spirits in the sciences.[19] Similarly, unbelievers are convinced that they have done enough if they, for the sake of society,[20] show outward religiosity, but the nature of their theses are completely opposed to Christian doctrine.

The nature of unbelief itself effectuates this, but the rejection of the rightful impact of Christianity on the sciences by Christians themselves is doubly lamentable. And by "Christians" in this case, I do not only mean those for whom Christ is merely a teacher, reformer, or philosopher but not a God and Savior, or those who confess with the mouth what they have never sought nor believed, or even those who express a cultural religiosity. No, I mean even Christians who have a genuine and undoubted faith yet become

---

[19] What Groen notes here concerning medieval scholars is highly relevant to the current discussions regarding Radical Two-Kingdom Theology, often described by its advocates as Reformed Two Kingdoms. While Classical Two-Kingdom Theology, as understood within the framework of the Protestant Reformation, did not allow for such a dichotomy between the church/spiritual realm and society/natural realm, Groen here points out that there was indeed a view commonly held during the late medieval times that dichotomized the spiritual and natural realms to such an extent that God's Law as revealed throughout Scripture only applied to the former.

[20] *Groen: They often do this for their own sake. Unbelievers, for the sake of veiling their outright rejection of Christianity, have often exhibited a twisted eccentricity. A fine example of this is Rousseau. Others have twisted Christianity into a religion that suits their own desires, to the extent that nothing remains of the true gospel. This was the modus operandi of Kant.*

annoyed as soon as the authority of God's Word is recognized in the practice of the sciences. How is this phenomenon to be explained?

This is due to the feebleness of Christians who often offer such little resistance to the spirit of the age. This is why in an anti-Christian age, so much of what ought to be defended by Christians is willingly sacrificed by most. Unbelief sanctions the idea that one can be a Christian and yet regard religion, politics, and science to be completely separable. Thereby the agenda of godlessness is fully vindicated. It becomes the central axiom that science must be kept free or purified from religious "interference"—an axiom that is so incompatible with Christianity that those who confess it only remain Christian by virtue of their fortunate inconsistency. The absurdity of forsaking Christianity in the sciences while maintaining it in the church is often the result of cowardice and often due to an implicit acceptance of the supremacy of unbelief. Those who adhere to and practice this believe that they have found the best way to be counted among the so-called civilized and enlightened people of our age without forsaking the faith. Thereby many of the fiercest proponents of godless philosophies themselves—often without realizing the consequences—have been Christians because they seek exculpation for their adherence to the gospel by means of their scientific unbelief.

In this way, Christians are often swept away by anti-Christian prejudice. But those who could previously be excused because they could not see the full implications of the spirit of this age are now without excuse. The Christian worldview has been vindicated by the fruitlessness and depravity of the anti-Christian view. That divine revelation should reign supreme in the sciences is evidenced by the confusion and violence that now characterize the national life of the misled and agonized nations that have forsaken Christian principles. Let us always continue to strive to be ready with an answer against the deceptions of the time, and let us never forsake the standpoint of the gospel, which remains relevant for every age.

2
Revelation

It is vital that the principles of any science, including those of politics and international law, accord with Scripture, or at least that they are not opposed to it. This is evident to all those who have embraced those truths which the Christian Church acknowledges to be divine revelation.[21] But what must be understood by "revelation" or "Christianity" or "Christian Church"? In different times, the claim that "we are Protestant Christians" would have been sufficient. Nowadays there are various and even contradictory meanings attached to these same words. And in terms of religion, many now make no distinction between a genuine, living faith on the one hand and madness or fanaticism on the other. Thus we are now often compelled, as I am here, to provide a comprehensive explanation of the meaning of these words.

---

[21] Groen here applies the Reformation's principle of *Sola Scriptura* to the sphere of politics and international law. While Scripture can never be the source of all knowledge, it is the ultimate standard of all truth and ethics, and all that is opposed to it ought to be rejected.

Christianity

Christianity is the source of all religious enlightenment. The restoration of the image of God in fallen man and redemption through faith in Christ and Him crucified is the central focus of the content of revelation, and these ideas are found, in varying degrees, most often in a hybrid and corrupted form, sometimes more and sometimes less clearly, in all other religions. True religion is found solely in the Christian Church; however, under various names and at various times, the essence has always remained the same.[22] The religion of the patriarchs, the ancient Israelites and the Christian Church, both prior to and after the Reformation, is one and the same.

The many heresies are the result of the embezzlement of revealed truths by the wrong insights and passions of fallen men. Whatever truths can be observed in the sects are the result of that which is truly Christian and which has remained in them, effectuated by the light that pierces the fog.

The natural, pagan, Islamic, and Deist religions originated but deviated from the true religion that has been revealed. Some claim that man has always had an innate knowledge of an Eternal Being or God, and that Christianity was a necessary addition to this insufficient original knowledge. This claim is simply too unhistorical to deserve any extensive refutation. People have received their knowledge of God from either their ancestors or from God Himself, but they certainly did not discover it through their own

---

[22] *Groen: "This Holy Catholic Church has existed from the beginning of the world, and will last until the end, which is evident from this, that Christ is an eternal King, which, without subjects, cannot be." —Belgic Confession, Article 27.*

ingenuity.[23] Some claim that humanity, if left to itself, would be able to come to the knowledge of the central truths of religion and morality. But the fact is that the natural religion of a depraved sinner is enmity against God. If we observe what depraved humans become through apostasy, we can only imagine what they could be without any light of revelation.

The truths ascribed to natural religion are supposedly confirmed by reason and this natural religion is said to be rational. How much wisdom, they claim, was not known by the ancient philosophers! Undoubtedly, but these basic truths were derived from the traditional religion of their ancestors. Their highest wisdom consisted in their ability to, at times, distinguish these truths of the religion originally revealed from the froth of their national superstitions and the doctrines originating from their priests.[24]

---

[23] Here Groen takes a decisively anti-rationalist stance in favor of what can only be described as Christian Historicism in the tradition of the *Historische Schule* of the German conservative Friedrich Carl von Savigny (1779–1861). This school had a major impact on Groen's thought and was characterized by a rejection of natural law as received through natural reason, in favor of a historicist and traditionalist explanation for the reality of human knowledge.

[24] *Groen: Examples include the unity of God and the immortality of the soul. Wittenbach denied this in his works on this topic. He wanted to credit humanity and its nature for coming to the knowledge of these truths. He vigorously reproached those who credit the remnants of the religion of Moses for this while he dodged the central question: not if the ancient philosophers ever read any part of Holy Scripture, but whether they received it by means of an oral tradition that originated from the same original divine revelation, of which the Bible contains the original record and by which it is preserved. The source of the pagan knowledge of God did not consist in the eminence of human*

Religion is traditional. Knowledge of the true God could not arise with the rough natural man, as the false philosophies propose. We see this with nations where the knowledge of God has almost been completely lost. Without help, they exhibit virtually no progress. Various religions have arisen from fear, gratitude, awe, and politics, and reflect true religion insofar as it has been transmitted and cast into the new forms. But the origin of true religion cannot be found with mankind itself. It is the same with language. A variety of languages exist. But a language itself is the product of tradition. The similarities between religions are the necessary result of the unity of God and mankind. What the Bible teaches in this regard is vindicated by history. We would have been able to trace the genealogy of religions had it not been that so much historical data has been lost. Even in Fetishism, where people kneel before wood, stone, or animals, there remains a spark of true religion, so that even the greatest degeneration itself bears witness to its glorious origins.

Pagan religions originated from the influence of sin, in that the lie followed the truth. But the mark of the common origin of religions has been preserved in these religions themselves. The myths contain some remnants of basic truths of revelation, which have admittedly become almost unrecognizable by eccentric additions that have also robbed these truths of their strength and power. Nonetheless, they bear witness of the truth, even if it is suppressed: one god, one evil spirit, an original human condition of innocence and thereafter of depravity and faithlessness, a redeemer,

---

nature but rather in the fact that God had revealed Himself to them. Ο Θέος ἀύτος εφανέρωσε: "God has revealed Himself."

and a period of restoration—these characteristics have been imprinted in the collective memory of the nations. The sacrifices, the slaughtering of humans on the altar, the penance through pain that the Hindus inflict upon themselves—these are all reminiscent of the revelation that God's wrath rests upon mankind and that only through a bloody sacrifice in which humanity participates can this be atoned for. In the false religions, there is not only an emphasis on their distinct heresies but also upon that which has remained, albeit in a veiled form, of the originally revealed truths. Thereby every religion, in contradistinction to complete irreligiosity, has at some stage served the well-being of the state and public morals, until it became gravely corrupted and its truths were destroyed by the superstitions of the masses, the deception of the priests, and the arguments of philosophers.

Employing the growth of Islam as an argument against Christianity bears witness to a lack of historical understanding. All that is good in Islam has been borrowed from the revelation of the God of the Bible: by virtue of its Christian elements, Islam has managed to exercise a surprising amount of influence on the history of the world. The more truth a lie contains, the greater impact and strength it has. The reason that such a large part of the world has submitted to Muhammad's doctrine is because he, in the midst of the great degeneration of the East, returned to some elements of the revelation, even if he completely denied its essence.

As strange as this may seem to some, the fact of the matter is that even the deism and atheism of the eighteenth century, yes, even their false doctrines regarding morality, immortality, liberty, and equality, were indirectly derived from revelation.[25] But separated from core truths and first principles, they became false and depraved,   although, they are both wholesome and undeniable in proper relation to the highest truth. By virtue of their Christian elements, deism and atheism have managed to conquer a Christianity that was Christian in name only—a religion that, through superstition, lifeless worship, and arbitrariness, had become powerless in most countries.

A unity of religions only exists in as much as there are unadulterated remnants of their common origin in the original revelation.[26] But there is only one true

---

[25] *Groen: In comparing Christianity and the false philosophy, it is often forgotten that everything that the latter boasts about, even if distorted, is originally derived from divine revelation. The comment of Neander is true: "The ideas of universal human rights, of religious liberty, and liberty of conscience was completely alien to the ancients and it was only through the light of the gospel that it has been revealed." With regard to that in which the philosophers of the eighteenth century excelled beyond Plato, Cicero, and Plutarch, it was certainly not by virtue of their own ingenuity.*

[26] *Groen: The commentary on Ephesians 2:12 in the Statenvertaling Bible reads: "If they do not know the Son, they do not know the Father either." At the end of this chapter, I provide an example of the Christian view of politics and international law. What does, many will ask, original sin have to do with politics? Quite a lot, the Belgic Confession answers in article 36: "God, because of the depravity of mankind, hath appointed kings, princes, and magistrates." The necessity of a legitimate authority rests on the depravity of all of mankind. If you regard our pitiful condition not as the result of Adam's sin but as having come through societal institutions, the idea that the nations should be redeemed through improved governance follows. Governments then come to be seen as guardians whose authority will only cease once a higher level of*

religion by which the broken line to the original revelation can be recovered. There is only one Redeemer, one Name by which one can be saved, one Christ, outside of which people live without God in the world.

Protestantism

The strength of the term "Protestantism" lies in it being defined from a Christian perspective, since it would otherwise not be a suitable name. Many who call themselves "protestors" or "protestants" have nothing in common with Christian Protestantism. They are often unbelievers or skeptics who protest against the truths of Christianity just as much as the Protestant Christian does against the heresies of the Roman Catholic Church.

Protestantism, or the basis of the blessed Church Reformation, is Christianity at war with unchristian doctrine, by which Rome had forsaken the ancient and catholic faith. But this polemic focus remained too narrow, and when the insufficiency of the expression could no longer be supplemented by a Christian spirit, even the non-Christian, being a non-Catholic, identified under the banner of Protestantism. This would not have happened if the different Protestant Churches had remained true to the original principles of the apostolic and orthodox catholic faith.[27] But the

---

enlightenment and civilization has been achieved. Deliverance is sought through political forms and tricks, not in a return to true religion and morality. And because of the rejection of this single biblical truth, people have been deceived by the heresies of the sophists and illuminists, which have proven fatal for the nations of Europe.

[27] For Groen, it is vitally important to distinguish the Protestant Reformation from the revolutions that he so

Protestant Churches themselves have been corrupted by scientific and practical unbelief and decay. Rationalism, which makes religious truths dependent upon reason, as well as Neology,[28] which twists the Bible into an anti-biblical system, have brought about a kind of Protestantism as far removed from the blessed Reformation as light is from darkness, as divine authority is from human arbitrariness, as heaven is from earth or, rather, as heaven is from hell. Because of the united development of European civilization, this evil has had an impact everywhere on the continent, and everyone who loves Christian truth agrees that we must resist this anti-Christian Protestantism (which strives for dominance under the veil of tolerance) everywhere it rears its ugly head.

The foundation of Protestantism must be Christianity. Protesting is only good if it is done on the basis of and in accordance with God's Word. On this faith all protests against superstition and unbelief must be based. It is because they were steadfast Christians that Luther and Calvin were Protestants. This solid foundation must never be forsaken if we are to remain steadfast against the heresies of Rome and if Protestantism is to be vindicated against reproaches.

Protestantism is unjustly called, in relation to Rome, a new doctrine. The doctrine of the gospel is as old as Christianity itself, and Protestantism was in the

---

vehemently opposed. During his own time, many of his anti-revolutionary allies were conservative Roman Catholics who blamed the Protestant Reformation for the Enlightenment and the French Revolution. Refuting this false notion was integral to Groen's aim of legitimizing his distinctly Calvinist anti-revolutionary theory.

[28] During this time, "Neology" was the term commonly used to refer to the rationalist theology prevalent in Germany during the eighteenth century (see footnote 31).

church from the beginning. From early on, it was necessary to expressly oppose such heresies such as those that were later defended by Rome. Thus, in this sense, St. Paul and St. Peter were also Protestants.[29] The Church of Rome had, for many ages, a blessed impact in terms of preserving and expanding the Christian faith. The impact that the church hierarchy and the authority of popes had on kings and nations, in terms of enlightenment, liberty, and civilization, was also generally positive. However, Roman Catholics cannot claim this earlier positive impact of the church exclusively as their own. The Church of Rome was at first completely, and after that partially, Protestant. The heresies that they eventually proclaimed were initially resisted by all and then by many, even in the midst of persecution and the threat of being burnt at the stake. When darkness became common, God desired to bring about a new light over Christendom. The Protestants split from the seat of unchristian superstition, not because they did not belong to the Catholic Church, but because they refused to forsake the truth of the gospel and stood steadfast against those who distorted Catholic truth. Protestantism is the continuation of the Apostolic-Catholic Church of which the so-called Roman Catholic Church, as it had existed from the fifteenth century and perhaps earlier, was a distortion. The progress made by the Reformation was in essence a return to that which the people had forsaken. The change brought about by Protestantism amounted to essentially reclaiming that which the people had come to reject. Papism is new and Protestantism is old.

Catholicism and Protestantism were one at first and so whenever they are contrasted, it can only be

---

[29] *Groen: 1 Peter 5:1-4; Acts 15:22.*

from the time that Catholicism was redefined at the Council of Trent. Those Protestant Churches that have remained true to their confession belong to the true Catholic Church, from which the Church of Rome has separated itself as a lapsed sect.

What is it that separates Protestantism from Roman Catholicism since this split? The differences are often either downplayed or exaggerated. The first is because many are either ignorant about the differences or desire not to see them. Many have made much of images, priestly celibacy, indulgences, the hierarchy, and the authority of the pope—which are matters of lesser importance, or which have already been addressed, or with regard to which many Roman Catholics, even in the time of Erasmus, have desired reform. Few recognize the importance of building upon the foundation of the Bible alone, of justification by grace alone, of Christ as the only Head of the Church, by whose Spirit she is guided and preserved. This is partially due to the disregard for religious truths, which, by virtue of the growth of unbelief, has also become characteristic among those who are not unbelievers. This reveals an utter ignorance of the essence and value of the Reformation and amounts to a misrepresentation of the spirit of our ancestors,[30] which focused on the preservation of the essence of saving faith.

No, the difference between Protestants and Catholics pertains to the essence of the matter and, as long as the Roman Church maintains its characteristics, no unification is possible.

---

[30] Their actions are often explained solely in terms of a love for liberty and privileges rather than the gospel. In this way, they are misrepresented as modern liberals.

But the differences are often also exaggerated, and some often completely disregard the similarities. People often loathe the Roman Church for the Christian truth it proclaims. The church has, notwithstanding its superstition, not forsaken faith in Christ. Therefore, the divide between the Catholics and Protestants is smaller than the divide between us and any religion that rejects the gospel or only embraces a semblance thereof for the sake of an anti-Christian agenda.

In light of the prevalence of Rationalism and Neology,[31] it can be explained why such a large number of people forsake Protestantism for the Roman Catholic Church. Many Protestants, who would have remained true to the foundations of the Reformation, would rather go where Christ is preached than where He is preached away. They flee unbelief, albeit into the lap of the Roman Church! It is, however, rather strange that many knowledgeable men, even those with an excellent knowledge of history, confuse the degeneration of Protestant doctrine with true Protestantism itself. This is often attributed to their particular religious and political sentiments. But it is certain that, if they sought a more solid foundation for political theory by means of their transition, they have missed the mark. Just as a false Protestantism despises

---

[31] Editor's Note: Neology, a rationalistic version of Christianity, prioritizes reason over revelation to understand religious truth, unlike the Middle Ages when revelation had higher authority over reason. It also de-emphasized tradition, thus aligning itself with political liberalism. Lutheran philosophers like Christian Wolff and Johann Salomo Semler led the shift toward rejecting miracles and divine revelation, twisting Christianity into a natural religion. Neology dominated in the eighteenth century, creating a significant conservative/liberal divide in the Lutheran church.

true authority, only true Protestantism honors, confirms, and sanctifies legitimate authority.[32] Maintaining the Christian truth is the only guarantee against proselytism toward the Roman Church, yet partial or full neo-Protestantism actually effectuates this.

Our Christian responsibility toward the Roman Catholic Church entails that we defend her against unbelief, something for which there is nowadays ample opportunity. Since Christ is attacked through her, the Roman Church must be defended by Protestants. But this does not entail becoming Roman Catholic. Maintaining a principle does not imply approval of a theological system in which these principles are not rightly understood or rightly applied. We aren't Romish, but we appreciate those in the Roman Church who are Christians. Christ is our Lord. In Him, Protestants and Catholics have a common interest and common ground in the fight against unbelief. Both sides unfortunately downplay this common ground. The Roman Church has allied herself with the liberals against the Protestants.[33] What foolishness! This alliance alone has been the cause of much apostasy from the Roman Church. Because of fortunate circumstances, the liberal doctrines, which are incompatible with faith in Christ, have not been

---

[32] Groen highlights the anti-revolutionary character of Protestantism. While the liberal revolutionaries oppose and overthrow legitimate authority, Protestantism seeks to maintain the authority of God and His revelation over and against man-made religion that essentially constitutes rebellion against divine authority.

[33] Most likely, Groen has the Roman Catholic Church in the Netherlands and Belgium in mind, which, at the time, supported the liberals who drove the Belgian Revolution in 1830.

consistently accepted or applied within the Roman Catholic Church. The Protestants are also guilty of rejoicing over the humiliation of the Roman Catholic Church at the hands of the liberals as if they believe that unbelief would serve as a passage toward true faith. An expectation no less bizarre than the idea that the nations would be brought to true liberty and legitimate authority by means of complete anarchy. The opposite is true: instead of drawing closer to the truth, they drift further away. Those within the Roman Church only need to become convinced that works salvation is a fallacy and that church authorities are fallible, but they already recognize the reality of sin and the necessity of fleeing to Christ for salvation. With unbelievers or rationalists, one also has to deal with self-righteousness, self-interest, and pride—evils that are less easily conquered than superstition.

The liberalization of a Roman Catholic country is by no means a victory for the Protestant Church. I would rather have them maintain their superstition than to decline in complete unbelief. We ought to honor their flawed religiosity for as long as there is nothing better that can take its place. Superstition itself presupposes the existence of some faith, and therein lies the transition point to true faith.[34]

Knowledge of what is truly Protestantism is necessary to refute the reproaches against the Reformation. These reproaches are often based on the false assumption that Protestantism desired unlimited liberty of free study and expression. Roman Catholics often point to Neology, a liberal and rationalist theology, as proof that Protestantism allowed heresies

---

[34] *Groen: As Bilderdijk noted: "Even the roughest versions of Christian doctrine contain more truth than a false philosophy."*

to become axiomata. According to this interpretation, the Reformation was the beginning of the decline, the seed for atheistic philosophy, and the preparation for the revolutionary era. But only a little knowledge of history is needed to disprove this interpretation.

The Reformers did not stand on the foundation of unbelief and did not advocate the supremacy of reason. Through faith, they desired that the doctrines of the church be tested in light of the infallible Word of God.

The right to study theology for oneself was granted by the Reformation, but in practice, it was applied in a very different way than what it is reproached for. For any given human being the right to study is granted notwithstanding any other rights of any other person. Thus, it follows that no one can violate conscience by forcing his beliefs or worldview upon another. Conversion by means of an inquisition or burning at the stake is understandable when one wrongly makes salvation dependent upon membership in a visible church, yet since God is served in spirit and in truth, forced conversions have no place.

For Christians, the right to study is limited within the confines of revelation. Precisely because we are bound to the doctrines of Scripture, we necessarily compare it to all that is proposed to us on the basis of any human authority. The Bible is the standard. Hereby, church councils and church doctrines are not robbed of their authority, but they are arranged according to the highest law of the Christian Church. In principle, all members of a Christian Church are bound to respect the foundational law of that church. Hereunto, the pastors ought to be even more respectful, since, if they are not subject to the authority of the church, their own authority becomes completely arbitrary. A declaration of unconditional faith in the Bible is required for every Christian. A declaration regarding one's position on the authority of the Bible and its contents is required of its members by all Protestant denominations. The reproach that the Reformation's adoption of confessions amounts to forsaking the ancient doctrines has been made a thousand times before.[35] It is the opponents of true Protestantism that advocate the doctrine of unbelief. The Reformers were not opposed to the authority of church doctrine but stood against the church's independence from the Bible.[36] By not continuing to

---

[35] *Groen: Undoubtedly the composers of the Protestant confessions were most familiar with the writings of the church fathers like Augustine, and others like Bernard of Clairvaux, and despite the reproach that they disregarded the fathers, they (Melanchthon, Calvin, Guido de Bres, and others) generally had the same attitude as Luther when he wrote: "The Word of God is above all. When I stand upon the majestic authority of the Divine Word, I do not worry if Augustine or Cyprian stands against me. God cannot err and cannot lie. Augustine and Cyprian and all the other fathers could err, and did err." The nature and value of the confessions have been beautifully explained by Mr. van der Kemp's refutation of Hofstede de Groot. Such expositions are most valuable whenever they are enticed by heresy. Bilderdijk also wrote that "those who advocate doctrines in the church that are opposed to the confessions—they are the intolerant, the intruders, the violators of both civil rights and consciences." It is especially abominable when one expects others to follow the decisions of church councils while maintaining the liberty not to do so for oneself: a false balance or measure is an abomination to the Lord.*

[36] *Groen: They desired to maintain relations—the confessions were declarations to both friend and foe. The Protestants thereby declared what they considered to be biblical and Christian. They did this because they refused to tolerate anything unchristian in the midst of their assemblies. This observation by Burke is, in terms of the gist of it, also applicable to countries other than England: "Our predecessors in legislation were not so irrational (not to say impious) as to form an operose ecclesiastical establishment,*

test their confessions against Scripture, many Protestants have become inconsistent. An unconditional faith in the truths of Scripture does not preclude writing down those very truths or creating a church motto, but it does entail leaving any denomination whose confession is opposed to the Word of God. However, some claim that an unconditional faith in the Bible, without confessions, is sufficient for the Protestant Church. For individuals this may have been true, but it is certainly not true for churches. The Bible! Oh, everyone is happy with the Bible because each can justify his own religion from the Bible. Liberal Protestants also claim faith in the Bible and maintain its expressions but provide a new meaning to its every word. Every heretic has his verse and even the Romanists claim that the infallibility of the pope is based in the Holy Scriptures. Declaring the Bible to be the only standard without any further explanation is underestimating the role of reason in religious matters. The Bible is infallible, the human mind isn't. The mind must be illuminated in order to be able to clearly see the truths of our faith. The Bible will always be explained in different and contradictory ways. Thus, if in the church, the community of

---

and even to render the state itself in some degree subservient to it, when their religion (if such it may be called) was nothing but a mere negation of some other; without any positive idea either of doctrine, discipline, worship and morals, in the scheme which they professed themselves, and which they imposed upon others, even under penalties and incapacities. No! No! This never could have been done even by reasonable atheists." The history of the early days of the Dutch Protestant Church also has manifest examples of tolerance toward Roman Catholics. Thereafter, if there had been examples to the contrary, it was because Dutch Catholics were, at the time, not unjustly viewed as enemies of the state.

believers, there is no rule of faith, there will be no church but instead complete confusion or, at the very least, complete submission to the ideas of the clergy and the academics—a true anarchy of opinions and a thousand papacies.

The foundation of the Reformation was by no means unbridled liberty. They had, even in embracing liberty of conscience, limited freedom of expression within the bounds of foundational truths.[37] They desired unity and perseverance along with free development.

Protestantism, many say, is the doctrine of unbelief, confusion, idleness, revolt, and slavery.

A doctrine of unbelief? The Reformation actually halted the march of unbelief. Too often she has been reduced to a doctrine fighting superstition. It is often forgotten that by the sixteenth century, doubt and atheism had already gained a foothold in the Roman Church.[38] The Reformation was like a steadfast wall in opposing this. The later histories of France and England show that the rise of atheistic philosophy stands in an evident relation to the Roman Catholicism that preceded it. Unbelief's most spectacular rise was in countries where Roman Catholicism remained dominant, or where the spirit of the Reformation had been quenched by a dead orthodoxy.

A doctrine of confusion? A thousand sects, they say, rose up—all claiming allegiance to God's Word.

[37] Unlike his Neo-Calvinist successors Abraham Kuyper and Herman Bavinck, Groen did not advocate freedom of religion or pluralism in the public domain. In his *Handboek der Geschiedenis van het Vaderland* (Amsterdam: Höveker, 1852), page 73, he insists that a Christian government ought to use "legal means to punish blasphemy."

[38] *Groen: The Protestant desire to search the Scriptures is rooted in the desire to believe God and His Word.*

The existence of distortions and heresies in no way negates the unity of the Protestant Church, just like the heresies of Arius and Socinus did not destroy the Roman Church. The divisions are less visible in the Roman Church because they adhere to a kind of leniency in doctrine completely foreign to orthodox Protestantism.

The Protestants do not desire the unity of the faith any less than the Roman Catholics do. They advocate submission to the doctrine of the church because it is biblical, and submission to the Bible because it is divine.

The unity must be seen in its diversity. It isn't difficult to achieve unity in the Roman Catholic manner. Unconditional decrees regarding the faith are left to church councils, and that over which doubt exists and which ought to be investigated is, for the sake of unity, arbitrarily determined. The Reformers desired no unity at the cost of truth and no unity sanctioned by human authority. There was a diversity of views on a number of theological matters but also unity and agreement. It is strange that many enemies of Protestantism so often focus sharply on its differences in terms of nonessential matters but not on its unity in terms of the essential matters.[39] If the impact of the differences had not been, in the heat of the moment, overemphasized, less division would have arisen, and Calvinists and Lutherans could have perhaps been united in one Evangelical Church. Wycliffe, Huss, Luther, Zwingli, Calvin, Spener, Whitefield, and Wesley preached the same doctrine:

---

[39] *Groen: Then Bossuet would have not found it difficult to also pen a* Histoire des Variations. *The similarities and agreements between the Protestant Confessions offer a striking proof of the fact that the Reformers were guided by the one Spirit and one Truth.*

total depravity, redemption by the blood of Christ, the necessity of regeneration and sanctification, and the voidness of self-righteousness—the same doctrine in all matters pertaining unto salvation.[40]

In unity with each other and the church of all ages, they built their doctrine upon the gospel and belonged to the catholic Christian Church, which is bound to no place, time, or denomination and whose unity is not dependent upon the governance of the pope but upon God's Word and Spirit—not a material unity, as with the Roman Church, but a spiritual unity.

But there are those who accuse Protestantism of leading to idleness in its disregard for good works. But what basis does this have? They point to what the Roman Church has done: She has decorated Europe with beautiful church buildings, monuments honoring the holiness of our ancestors, monasteries, and centers of science. She has launched innumerable charity efforts, revived the arts, and through her missionaries invited the whole world to partake of the blessings of the gospel. Her influence can be regarded as the foundation of European society.

But this is only the positive side of the matter: the abuse in the monasteries, the way in which the money was collected for the building of churches, and the fact that people were often converted under threat of fire and sword, all bear witness to the fact that there is also a dark side.

The Roman Church has had a useful and wholesome impact on society. But in the way she exists today, she does not have the right to claim this achievement as her own, exclusively. This was, after all,

---

[40] It must be said here that Groen's failure to take into account the very real differences and disputes between the various reformers in terms of the sacraments, ecclesiology, and even soteriology is a serious oversight on his part.

mostly achieved when she was not yet corrupted, and when there existed no Roman Church as opposed to the Evangelical or Protestant Church. Even in her depraved condition she has still positively contributed, it has to be admitted, while every dead Protestant Church slumbers on a faith without works: a false, dead faith. But the foundational principle of the Reformation was by no means a fruitless faith. Compare the public morals in England, Scotland, and the Netherlands from before and after the purification of the church; witness the greatness and achievements of even the small nations where the Reformation flourished; and don't forget the zeal of the missionary work and the great Bible distribution from the Protestant world over the past few decades. And even then there are still those who dare question whether the Protestant faith, if alive, does not reveal itself as the most illustrious treasure and in the most blessed fruit.

Some accuse Protestantism of amounting to a doctrine of revolt and slavery. These two do go together, since the same teaching that tolerates no legitimate authority also cultivates the kind of men that crawl before arbitrary power. Thus it is one and the same accusation. Well, then, one and the same defense will show that in truth Protestantism is a doctrine of both liberty and obedience.

What was the motto of the Reformation? Faith and obedience to God. Obedience unto God is a guarantee against revolt since God commands that authorities be respected. But obedience unto God is also a guarantee against the slavish dependence upon and tolerance of injustice. The very principle of obedience is noble and holy: submission is not based on self-serving interest but on duty; it is not based on what is pleasing unto man but what is pleasing unto God. God has also willed the recognition and respecting of all legal rights and liberties, so that the right to resist tyranny, regardless of how difficult this is to maintain within the proper bounds, cannot be denied unconditionally. To obey God rather than man guarantees that we are not even allowcd to do anything contrary to our duty toward Him. If these principles were at times disregarded and wrongly applied, neither Christianity in general nor Protestantism in particular are to blame. The fault of confessors cannot be laid at the door of the confession. Especially in this regard, men have been unfair toward Protestantism in general and Protestants in particular.[41] The history of the Reformation itself liberates it from this reproach. What had become of true liberty under the authority of the pope and the emperor? In which countries have there, over the past few centuries, been a most exquisite harmony between true authority and true liberty? In France, in Italy, in Spain, in Austria? Or was it in England, Switzerland, and here in the Netherlands?[42]

Yes, a true Protestantism that remains true to its foundations stands firm against all these reproaches.[43]

---

[41] *Groen: Luther is accused of stirring up revolution, while he in fact vigorously opposed chaos and illegitimacy. He is also accused of advocating slavery whenever he reproached the revolutionaries. The same accusation could perhaps have been hurled against the apostle Peter: compare 1 Peter 2:13 with Acts 4:19.*

[42] *Groen: Even in Protestant countries where there was much disunity, the confessors of the true gospel had been the true defenders of liberty. The Stuarts, who tended toward Catholicism, thought much of the rights of the crown and little of the rights of the people. The Revolution of 1688 was not only anti-Catholic but also in service of liberty. Here in the Netherlands, it has always been the orthodox Protestants who fought for liberty in both state and church.*

[43] *Groen: Maintaining Protestant principles is of the highest importance even for political philosophy. Wherever*

Mysticism

Mysticism: This is indeed a word that needs thorough clarification and contextualization. There is a degenerate mysticism that any Christian desiring to remain true to divine revelation must avoid, but the term itself has lamentably become a scare mechanism by which people are drawn from faith to rationalism, and from rationalism to the most depraved form of apostasy. These days it seems like anyone judges everyone who practices religion more devoutly than them to be a mystic—even the deist is considered by the atheist to be a dangerous religious fanatic. Many now categorize Christianity itself as a deplorable form of mysticism.

But, insofar as it deserves to be rejected, what is the source and nature of mysticism? It distorts the harmony between the elements of the human spirit. There is a separation and dichotomization of the mind and the heart, which generates either a rationalist or sentimentalist religion. The history of religion and philosophy shows that, whenever either of these are man-made, the tendency has been to jump between either of these extremes. Revelation alone is able to bring an end to this dichotomy, but despite the influence of the gospel, this tendency remains present

---

contrary philosophies take hold, the rights of either kings or the people (or both) are discarded. The government, if it recognizes no salvation outside of the Roman Church, becomes a servant of the pope, or, if it foolishly desires to rule independent of the Lord Christ, disregards the very rights of the King of kings Himself. Its people fall into either worldly tyranny or complete submission unto the Vatican. The popish system itself contains the very seed of the dangerous revolutionary political philosophy. And the revolutionaries have taught us exactly what becomes of politics outside of Christianity.

among many Christians—as soon as one departs from primitive superstition, he in turn descends into zealous emotionalism or a purely rationalist theology. In light of this, the nature, meaning, and value of mysticism are revealed.

Whenever feeling and imagination are counted higher than understanding and faith, religion is founded not upon revealed truths, the essence of reality, or acquired facts. However, Christianity is also a religion of the heart, which is in no way at odds with the mind or with logic. But what then are the marks by which true Christianity can be distinguished from either rationalism or mysticism?

I'll mention three. Firstly, unconditional submission to Holy Scripture: The Christian unconditionally accepts its truths, while the mystic submits to his own feelings and the rationalist to his own mind. The desire of the Christian is to be guided by God's Word and Spirit and to be reconciled with God through Christ, while the mystic desires reconciliation with the Supreme Being, even outside of Christ, based on his own emotions and excitement, and the rationalist regards all notions of reconciliation with God as mere dreams and illusions.

And thus we see where true redemption lies: not in rationalism, which suppresses all faith and emotion in the name of cold cognitivism; and not in the external forms of a dead orthodoxy, which gives preference to the emotional faculties of the human spirit; but in the faithful submission to the revelation of God. By means of Scripture, the Spirit of God takes our entire being captive to Himself and unifies us with Christ, by which we learn to love God with all our heart, soul, and mind.[44]

One more word about politics and international law. It isn't strange that all that reeks of Christianity is now discarded by many as zealotry and exaggerated mysticism. Let us strive not to be swept away by either emotions and imagination or unbelief and rationalism. It is better to be accused of zealotry by non-Christians or by Christians who are disloyal to the principles of their religion than to advocate a political theory, the very first principle of which amounts to forsaking the highest truth.

---

[44] *Groen: Borger's work on mysticism now enjoys almost unconditional authority in the Netherlands. And no wonder. The combination of his treatment of reason and knowledge as well as his exceptional rhetoric, combined with his German philosophy, is something that cannot be found in many sources. Nonetheless, it seems as though his treatment of this philosophy is, at times, rather weak, especially when he describes the thought of Schelling. Schelling does not deserve to be grouped with the likes of Fichte, who counts among those whom van der Palm describes as "building empty abstractions upon barbaric rhetoric and robs us of all that we have ever believed or held dear, and grants us the liberty to maintain traditional religious terminology, as long as we are willing to sacrifice the essence of the matter."*

3
Philosophy[45]

Many people now exhibit an aversion to philosophy in general. This is because false philosophy has effectuated a prejudice against true philosophy. Revelation, philosophy, and history form one complete whole.[46] By virtue of the influence of unbelief, philosophy has become pernicious to the Christian and to everyone who desires true knowledge of history.[47]

---

[45] *Groen: In this chapter, more than elsewhere in this book, I ask the reader to be a generous judge. There are greater experts in this particular field than I count myself to be, and I would love to see the ideas I propose here be more clearly and thoroughly explained and verified.*

[46] *Groen: "Theology is the highest synthesis of philosophy and history." —Schelling.*

[47] *Groen: The new philosophy is, in fact, very anti-philosophical. "The abstractions, which they like to call Enlightenment, stand opposed to true philosophy. The French sophists have, in all sciences, usurped the name of philosophers. We ought not to acknowledge them as true philosophers." Plato himself, who desired to see philosophers govern the state, would not have honored the French sophists with the title of philosophers.*

Philosophy has always been inseparable and dependent upon religion. Defective religious principles have always effectuated a defective philosophy. Christianity alone can be the foundation of true philosophy.

The relationship between religion and philosophy is obvious and has always been acknowledged. The highest philosophy is the knowledge of God—therein lies its very root and principle.[48] Philosophy is the highest science since it occupies itself with the essence of reality—how can it lead us anywhere but to the knowledge of God?

Holy Scripture teaches that knowing and fearing God, as He has revealed Himself in Christ, is the principle of wisdom. It is only because unbelief has reigned for an extended period of time that a separation between Christianity and philosophy has become possible at all.[49] This principle of the unity of religion and philosophy is even found among the pagans. The deeper you delve into history, the clearer the unity between religion and philosophy becomes. Only later did a tension arise between those who continued to adhere to their tribal religion, which had through time distorted the original ideas of revelation, and the philosophers, who felt nothing for these depraved remnants of the original truths. But even in

---

[48] *Groen: Cicero writes that "philosophy must train us to worship the gods." But contrary to what he believed, the reality is that philosophy does not beget religion, but true religion begets true philosophy.*

[49] Groen is an advocate of a distinctly Christian philosophy as the only true philosophical system based upon the central presupposition that the Triune God has infallibly revealed Himself in Scripture, and that belief in this revelation is required to accurately interpret the things of the natural world in terms of their interrelationship as well as the genesiology, ontology, and teleology of each.

such cases, the philosopher's ideas were based in his conception of God—that is, in his religion.

There is a so-called philosophy that seeks to resist all religious truth and effectively makes apostasy its foundational principle. But even this point of departure proves the intrinsic connection between religion and philosophy. The atheist has made an idol of himself and placed himself at the center—where God belongs. They have made the nonexistence of all that is not sensually observable their central presupposition. They are inescapably necessitated to openly reveal their unbelief and have thereby unintentionally shown philosophy to be inseparable from religion.

Since philosophy is a result of religion, a false religion always begets a false philosophy. All philosophical systems, apart from Christian philosophy, are flawed and false. This insufficiency, and this corruption of the highest truth, has revealed itself in half-truths and contradictions, which can only be harmonized by the light of the gospel.

Among the ancient nations we need to look no further than the Greeks, who rank above all the rest. Their philosophers taught many outstanding truths. But even in their case, a higher enlightenment must be recognized. The influence of myths, originating from the Greeks themselves but also from the nations to their east, and the merits of their philosophy lie more in the remnants of true revelation than in their own designs. The truth in Greek philosophy is a credit to its self-purification from the traditions of idolatry and superstition, not to its rational endeavors.[50] Besides,

---

[50] Groen here echoes one of Von Savigny's sentiments, which are distinctly characteristic of the *Historische Schule*—namely, that the truths contained in ancient philosophy should not be attributed to the right use of human reason but to the traditions that those philosophers maintained.

the Greek philosophers more often than not lack clarity, purity, completeness, and certainty.[51] Christianity, on the other hand, offers not only an explanation but a purification of pagan philosophy. Whatever truths may be known to the pagans, they have no ultimate standard or foundation for their doctrine or ethics. They may bear witness to the reality of human depravity, but they offer no explanation of its origin or of redemption. They may feel that there is a divide between Creator and creation, but they know not the Redeemer who gives meaning to all knowledge.[52]

[51] *Groen: No Greek philosopher stands quite as tall as Plato. In him, we can see how much and yet how little Greek philosophy achieved. Both Le Maistre and Schlegel credit him as offering a "preface to the gospel." He does, after all, proceed from God as foundation and traces in the traditions and oracles of the priests the features of revealed truths. He expresses a desire that can only be satisfied by Christianity. Thereby Greek philosophy ended up becoming, as Clement of Alexandria describes it, a steppingstone toward the gospel. Yet, regardless of how excellent and glorious the content of Plato's writings are, even when reading these, we need to heed the distinction between that which is the word of man and the Word of Him who has descended from Heaven. God is the ultimate standard, not humanity—and this is the stumbling block over which all the sophists, those of old and even more so those of our own time, fall. Where Christ is not known, God is not known.*
[52] *Groen: The achievements of the ancient Greeks and Romans are too often emphasized to the point of failing to mention their vices: superstition, cruelty, and immorality. Whenever their achievements are praised, too much is made of their external gloss and too little of the inherent depravity of their principles. Van Alphen writes: "Great are the achievements of the classical scholarship, but it is a shame that they are often glorified to the extent that one would gain the impression that nothing but Greek and Roman philosophy is needed to obtain salvation and that they are regarded as the source of true ethics." Truly unfortunate is anyone who is so addicted to ancient philosophy that they*

Therefore, in Greek philosophy itself, despite all its greatness and glory, lies the very seed of destruction: it descends into vain arguments and complete and utter doubt and uncertainty. It must be regarded, inasmuch as it destroyed the ancient national religions only to eventually descend into foolish self-glorification, as one of the main reasons for the decline and fall of ancient states.[53]

In the history of Christendom itself, there have actually been many philosophers who have been Christians but who were still by no means Christian

---

are content with it. If you read Cicero's book de Finibus, *it discusses the highest good. Well, then, what is that? Virtue or pleasure? The former is unachievable and the latter can only be an end of a philosophy that regards life itself as a party and immortality as an illusion. His* Tusculanae Questiones *has many valuable things to say about grief, depression, the desires of the human heart, and why the philosopher poses no threat to the ruler. Compare this to the gospel: it is like comparing the wizards of Egypt to Moses. A one-sided excitement about ancient philosophy had caused much damage in the past. The Reformation toned it down—for as long as the true spirit of the Reformation remained alive. Even in our own times, many are so enchanted by ancient philosophy that they have no regard for a genuinely Christian philosophy and civilization. Let us rather remain true to the advice offered by one of the bravest heroes and greatest kings of Sweden, Gustavus Vasa, to his son: "It is good to read the writings of the ancients and gain knowledge of the insights of their time, but place nothing ahead of God's Word. Herein you will find true doctrine and herein will be revealed to you true ethics and the greatest political theory."*

[53] *Groen: Heeren* [German historian Arnold Hermann Ludwig Heeren (1760–1842)] *mentions that among the most prominent causes for the fall of Greece was* "the sacrilege of the national religion. And it is true that the ideas of the philosophers had played a great part in this process, even if the best among them tried to hide this fact."

philosophers. They viewed their own research as completely unrelated to the Christian truths. There have also been many who, by virtue of their knowledge of the gospel, exceeded the wise philosophers of antiquity. Many, even if they weren't Christians at all, claimed to have been philosophers. In the eighteenth century, it seemed as though opposition to the gospel was the chief characteristic of the philosopher. This kind of philosophy was utterly deplorable and, had they not veiled their anti-Christian philosophy in the language of the gospel, many who are now dragged along would have seen the reprehensibility of their ideas. Yet, even the better elements in their philosophy are of no value given their anti-Christian framework and principles.

People are often in awe of the fact that the ancient philosophers had reached such fabulous insights even without the light of the gospel: equally unbelievable is the fact that the new philosophers have fallen so far despite their familiarity with the gospel. Breaking down without building up, or building up only to break down again immediately, bringing uncertainty in the sciences, anxiety, and despair of the mind and spirit—these are the chief characteristics of the new anti-Christian philosophy.[54]

---

[54] This is how Groen describes Enlightenment and post-Enlightenment philosophy, which had earlier been characterized by epistemological rationalism, and later by empiricism, and eventually a synthesis of the two as embodied by Immanuel Kant (1724–1804). In his magnum opus, *Unbelief and Revolution*, Groen is particularly critical of Kant, rejecting his ideas as leading to "a political theory in which a constitution ought to be sought through the artificial integration of individual interests with that of the whole, so that even in a society of demons, complete order, peace, and harmony could exist as long as the self-interest of each is rightly channeled." Groen condemns this idea as an

The history of non-Christian philosophy bears witness to a perpetual battle of differing sentiments whose incompatibility proves how little human reason, apart from revelation, can actually achieve.

Without divine help, unity in truth can never be achieved. Mankind, left to itself, sees only parts of truth, the better part of which it is ignorant of, and by virtue of devout attachment to that part that it has received, essentially distorts it.

There is a battle between mind and sentiment. The harmony between these two can only be restored by a higher principle, but as long as this does not happen, these forces are at war with each other—at times one wins and the other loses, and the one side of the scale rises when the other falls.

There is a battle between those for whom all should be subject to doubt and those who see all sentiments as affirmation. The one rightly desires certainty, but in looking for this in the human mind itself, he exhausts himself in mental discourses. The other realizes that the mind is no less subject to deception than the senses, and then proceeds to completely forsake the idea of certainty.

Man is both spiritual and material. No man-made argument can teach us how spirit and matter are united in us. The philosophers have often preferred either one or the other so that they have either materialized the spiritual or spiritualized the material. The result is either a spiritualism or a materialism.

For man, not understanding the origin of his depravity, he remains a great mystery to himself. He feels the desire and need for a higher existence, yet at

---

"arbitrary hypothesis" at odds with the reality of total depravity and our need for biblical revelation, also in the domain of civics (Groen van Prinsterer, *Ongeloof en Revolutie* [Leiden: S&J Luchtmans, 1847], 244).

the same time his tendencies often drag him in the opposite direction. At times he longs for a heavenly existence, at other times for the most earthly or animalistic one imaginable. One desires to rid himself of all desire, and the other indulges in pleasure. Two systems: one based in pride while the other is based in lust, while both cherish human depravity and are based in reprehensible selfishness. Stoicism or Epicureanism—this is where all worldviews outside of the gospel lead.

Revelation alone is the foundation of a holistic philosophy. It contains the highest and the only true philosophy.[55]

---

[55] *Groen: "The doctrines of Christianity, properly understood, is the highest philosophy, and alone teaches the truth regarding human nature." —August Tholück [1799–1877].*

The Christian philosopher [Carl Friedrich] Göschel [1784–1861] teaches that "in a time where a debate exists on whether a Christian philosophy is possible, our counterclaim is that there exists no genuine philosophy that is not Christian. In the so-called pagan philosophy of antiquity, as in the less impressive philosophy of our own time, there is only so much truth as there are echoes of Christianity. To separate philosophy from Christianity is to separate its contents and very purpose from truth."

The warning of the apostle in Colossians 2:3 is speaking with regard to the kind of philosophy that is not directed toward Christ, and for this reason the Statenvertaling rightly contains the following note on this passage: "hereby is not meant true philosophy, which is a gift from God, and is even a means by which to better understand and explain the Word of God, but rather sophistry." Therefore it was also recently observed in the Evangelische Kirchen-Zeitung *that: "To think that theology excludes philosophy is absurd, in as much as philosophy is understood to be the cultivation of ideas; but theology necessarily excludes the kind of philosophy that disregards the living God, as well as that which proposes ideas contrary to the Word of God."*

Only Christianity can solve that which remains an unsolvable mystery to philosophy and which contains the key to true wisdom and eternal salvation. Faith restores the harmony between reason and emotion. Revelation teaches us how to understand the human consciousness of both glory and misery. It provides the only solid foundation for principles.[56] It provides that which philosophy promises.[57]

Outside of Christianity there always existed an antagonism between religion and philosophy. And it cannot be otherwise, as pagan religion always comes to be increasingly viewed as superstition by the philosophers. Believing and knowing come to be seen as mutually exclusive. The Christian, however, acknowledges that faith and knowledge are one and the

---

[56] *Groen: Outside of Christianity, dualism is inevitable and people can only choose between heresies. Even among cultural Christians, whenever the Holy Scripture is forsaken as absolute standard, the inevitable choice becomes Pelagianism or Fatalism, works salvation or a religion without works, complete impotence or reliance upon human strength. The Christian, in remembering the words of Philippians 2:13, avoids both: "I can do all things through Christ who strengthens me." The man who relies upon his own human strength is, according to Luther, not unlike a drunken farmer who continually falls off his horse, first on the left and then on the right side. This falling off to one side and then the other is essentially the history of human philosophy.*

[57] Groen here advocates for a position on faith and reason that is akin to that of his forebears such as Anselm of Canterbury (1033–1109) and his successors such as Cornelius Van Til (1895–1987)—namely, that reason, though polluted by sin and therefore unable to come to thorough knowledge of God and the genesiological, ontological, and teleological nature of reality, is sanctified by faith and guided to proper understanding by the Holy Spirit.

same and that there exists a harmony between religion and philosophy, as both acknowledge revealed truth.

Christian philosophy, which has often been called Christianity applied,[58] contains the principles of knowledge and science.[59] She is the sun that enlightens the fields of human research. Every science, properly practiced, bears witness to the truth of revelation. If not, her very distortions and misconceptions, even

---

[58] Groen: *"Philosophy is applied theology, if it may be called as such. It is the means by which the ideas of revelation are applied to historical, experiential, and natural sciences."* — Schlegel

[59] Groen: *Science, if separated from religion, only serves to strengthen the power of human depravity and, if anything, worsens the corruption. It is not by mere cognitive knowledge, apart from revelation, that apostate nations again become civilized. "The root of all human progress is true religion." —Tholück*

It has often been said that in many ages past, science paved the way for Christianity. It may be true that by the providence of God this has at times been the case, but if you look at history, true enlightenment followed Christianity, not vice versa. True enlightenment only comes from true Christianity. This can also be seen via the influence of the Reformation. Science needs Christianity. For the sake of true knowledge, science needs to be practiced with a Christian spirit. In political science this can be shown without much effort. But this does not mean that each science is not independent. As Heeren describes it: "Reducing all science to religion is the view of the East. Like the Greeks we distance ourselves from such a perspective, thereby maintaining the true character of Western science." The independence of the sciences does not mean separation from religion, however, which is neither the view of the East nor the West. The independence of science does not entail autonomy, and while we desire no centralization, religion remains the heart of all science.

unintentional, reveal and honor the highest truth.[60] Proper research always leads back to the source of light and life.[61]

This holds doubly true for our own time. Anti-Christian and unchristian philosophy must be repelled. It is clear that they amount to a deceptive sham, while the true light of truth is found in the very revelation that they shun. Neither Romanism nor paganism was conquered by means of a philosophy itself but by means of the preaching of the gospel. Only as the Kingdom advances does the need for philosophical contemplation for the sake of advancing the cause of God's Word become necessary.[62]

---

[60] *Groen: For example, Christian political philosophy probably has few better proofs than the history of the revolutionary period.*

[61] *Groen: Even if research is conducted in an anti-Christian spirit, it produces evidence for Christianity.*

[62] *Groen: It is impossible to mold a Christian by means of philosophy alone. Besides, the philosophical method is not for everyone—in fact, it is ill-suited to most. It is most certainly true that the false philosophy of our age is the result of eighteenth-century sophistry and this should be corrected by means of true philosophy. But it must never be forgotten that false philosophy is the fruit of an underlying evil that must be addressed first. As has been rightly observed in the* Evangelische Kirchen-Zeitung: *"Minds have been corrupted by evil. Philosophy did not precede unbelief in France, but rather it was practical godlessness that produced the theoretical unbelief. The philosophical strain of unbelief will not be improved unless hearts are again convinced of their depravity, and for this to happen our prayers must be for the spirit of grace must be poured out over hearts from above."*

Christianity is, therefore, the only source of religious and philosophical enlightenment.[63] Now we must proceed to discuss the epistemic value of history.

---

[63] *Groen: Christian truth is the source of all good and true religious and philosophical convictions.*

4
History

This chapter contains two parts, the first of which addresses the relationship between revelation and history and the second the relationship between history and philosophy. Additionally, history's relationship to politics and international law will also be addressed.

Part 1: Revelation and History

In this section, I hope to convince the reader that Christ's redemptive work is at the center of history. Let us proceed to look at what history becomes outside of Christianity and thereafter look at what it truly is in light of the gospel.

The non-Christian view of history is fundamentally dissatisfactory. But it must also be admitted that the worldview of even the pagans contained certain appreciable views. They were, for example, aware of the divine influence on the world. They believed in personal deities, in judgments on kings and nations, and the religious writings of many Romans and Greeks indeed contain many valuable comments.[64] Nonetheless, their misconceptions regarding true providence are also often evident. They often resort to complete hopelessness because of their inability to acquire answers from heaven to their many questions.[65]

---

[64] Groen: *Examples include Homer and Herodotus. The famous Crenzer shows how all the works of Herodotus were shaped by his religious worldview. In Pindar and other dramatic poets there are many examples of religious poetry. Apart from the worship of the gods, the continual consultation of the oracles bears witness to their conviction that the fate of individuals and nations has been predetermined in heaven. This conviction not only had an impact on writers and poets but also on historians. The Greek historian Diodorus Siculus, who often pointed to the divine guidance of history, even called historians "servants of divine providence." The Christian historian is also a preacher of the gospel.*

[65] Groen: *The triumph of the wicked, the decline of nations seemingly destined for a glorious future, and the identification of evil in nature and history, which for many causes doubt regarding a benevolent Ruler of creation— these and many other questions they were unable to answer. The poet Claudian claimed that the fall of an evil man, one opposed to both mankind and the gods, reaffirmed his faith in divine providence. But as long as faith in the punishment of evildoers is limited to this life, this faith remains based on a shaky foundation. The truth—namely, that God governs—was distorted along with other distortions of divine revelation. Now they turned to a set fatalism, which could not be influenced or changed, not even by prayer. Good and evil were also viewed as two independently operating principles. And even in the midst of so much to cause atheism, they maintained their faith in a protecting providence, even if the nature of that providence remained unknown. Regarding that of which the Christian knows undoubtedly, they only remained hopeful and presumptuous.*

But it is much worse when apostasy from Christianity comes to shape the dominant view of history. By forsaking Christianity, the very notion of a personal God is abandoned, along with history's religious character. The true soul and drive of many historical figures are thereby completely ignored, and historical events and achievements are exclusively explained by means of secondary causes.[66] A

---

[66] *Groen: An example can be taken from the writings of someone who is not an enemy of Christianity by any stretch of the imagination. Europe has Christianity to thank for its supremacy over other parts of the world. Before it became civilized by virtue of the gospel, large parts of the continent remained uncultivated and were roamed by barbarian hordes. Yet how is this European supremacy explained by Heeren? What does he regard as the main cause of this spiritual and moral primacy? "Europe had a distinct indigenous character as white nations," he writes. The white nations are probably endowed with higher aptitudes, but in order to maintain a view in which the main reason for our advancement is sought in our physical traits, Heeren often regards as European the origin of things that must much rather be sought in Asia. Europe has been civilized by Asia: the Greek civilization was largely Eastern; the arts and sciences had, forgotten in Europe, flourished under the Arabs. And, as long as the dominance of Christianity was not appreciated, the people of the East would have been able to build a dominant civilization. Europe has been shaped by the gospel—our supremacy and civilization would have been lost if it had not found fertile soil in our part of the world. It would have been more reasonable had Heeren, even in appreciating the value of our racial characteristics, not concealed the impact of Christianity.*

Another example: The Revolution of 1688 undoubtedly had a Protestant character, but the historian Henry Hallam not only ignores this central characteristic but even laments "the danger of the Anglican Church from the bigotry of a hostile religion" and prefers to see in these events the

historiographic deism, completely different from the religion of the ancients, is now being pushed to the foreground. But who is the god of the deist and what can he do? It is, after all, an imaginary being, a product of the human mind, as vain as vanity itself. Such a man-made religion can barely address the mysteries of human existence, much less of history. The view of history derived from deism is not any less distorted than any other doctrines derived from false foundations.[67]

There is something else that amplifies our discontent with the deist in comparison to the ancient religious pagans. While the latter emphasized patriotism exclusively, the gospel sanctified this formerly selfish patriotism by adding to it a global citizenship of the Christian kingdom. Modern philosophy has preserved this cosmopolitan view, but in rejecting the gospel, they are, despite their increased knowledge and resources, left in despair as they, in all

---

triumph of the contemporary liberal or constitutional principles.

If there was ever a battle for the gospel, it was the Dutch Resistance, but historians have reduced this to a battle for rights and privileges. Sacrifices for the sake of Christianity seem to fall outside the scope of unchristian views of history. Great men are represented as cheaters and weak politicians. Prince William of Orange and Gustavus Adolphus are viewed as ambitious political pretenders. But once the witness of the primary sources is taken into consideration, denial of the historical role of the Christian religion in the actions of these men is impossible to deny.

[67] Groen here shows how religious presuppositions, being an inescapable part of all worldviews, inevitably shape the way people engage in scholarship. History is here used as an example, but in principle this also applies to all other sciences.

of world history, see only a metamorphosis without any order, purpose, or coherence.[68]

Indeed, it is unbearable to see world history as a scene of complete disorder and destruction. But this it has become through unbelief. Now that God has been rejected, an idol must be put in His place. The idea that there is a providential force or plan behind history has been discarded. Within the resultant incoherent and chaotic whole, a visible unity and order is desired. Thereby, as fruit of unbelief, a system of perfectibility is proposed.

Humanity, developed and cultured, strives, by detours, to what is regarded to be an achievable perfection. This is where the anti-Christian view of history leads: a system that is simultaneously anti-historical and anti-Christian.

The perfection of man can, according to the Bible, never be achieved by means of civilization and development, as this would presuppose an un-

---

[68] Here we see a reference to what R. J. Rushdoony would later describe as the "One-and-the-Many" problem continually presenting itself throughout the history of Western philosophy: "In much of Far Eastern thought, the problem of the one and the many no longer exists, since centuries ago resolution was made in favor of the one. The goal of being is then absorption into the one, and since particularity is unreal or even an illusion, it follows that history is unimportant. . . . In the West, philosophy has usually been dialectical, i.e., holding two antithetical principles in tension, such as form and matter in Greek philosophy, nature and grace in Scholasticism, and nature and freedom in modern thought. Because of this dialectical tension, it has been unable to rest content with a final solution as has the East. In the West, therefore, both 'realism' and 'nominalism,' the one and the many, have had their uneasy sway" (R. J. Rushdoony, *The One and the Many: Studies in the Philosophy of Order and Ultimacy* [Vallecito, CA: Ross House, 1971], 3–4).

depraved human nature, while Christianity teaches universal moral depravity.[69] The modern philosophy regards civilization as merely the grinding of a raw diamond, but Christianity teaches that humanity is completely under the bondage of sin, and that, unless a change in our disposition occurs, all civilization is merely veneering over evil by plastering the trenches. Revelation teaches us that humanity is incapable of any good in and of itself and that in order to become good, regeneration is needed. Our natural slavery to sin necessitates the need for redemption by a Higher Power.

The perfectibility of humanity as a whole is foreign to Scripture. In contradistinction it teaches difference and contrariety in status and eternal destination: faith and unbelief, redemption and damnation, heaven and hell; one people of God that will one day be perfected in Christ.[70] With this witness of revelation, the

---

[69] Groen: The Bible demands regeneration—"that you put off the old man which grows corrupt according to the deceitful lusts, and that you put on the new man which was created according to God, in true righteousness and holiness" (John 3:3, Ephesians 4:22, 24). The Bible emphasizes the necessity of the Holy Spirit and godly principles. This is the only way that humans can become perfect. "According to the Christian doctrine, the soul of man must be understood in terms of the image of God—of Christ—in man. The modern view identifies a pure human nature, an un-depraved reason, by which humanity is to be restored. The ideal is then the restoration of this pure and un-depraved humanity, which is understood to be the true humanity. Thereby the impact of the gospel on people is reduced to a fantasy." —Evangelische Kirchen-Zeitung. Scripture teaches that which the Reformed Confession explains—namely, that there is no perfectibility outside of Christ.

[70] Groen: The anti-Christian character of the doctrine of perfectibility is not so much seen in those passages of

Christian ought to be content, but it is not by any means redundant to show that history confirms the witness of Scripture regarding the evil inclinations of mankind.

Depravity is present in all countries at all times and under all forms of government, and even in the midst of all and any degrees of knowledge and education. Much has been said and written about the so-called untainted nations, among whom innocence and simplicity are said to be prevalent. This representation has also been defended by many firsthand reports. But among these natural, native peoples barely a shadow of moral sentiment can be found. Therefore their so-called "simplicity" would better be described as animalistic humanity.[71] On the other hand, the moral

---

Scripture that predict a future degeneration but those that address the essence of humanity and its need for redemption: "just as through one man sin entered the world, and death through sin, and thus death spread to all men, because all sinned; through one man's offense judgment came to all men, resulting in condemnation" (Romans 5:12, 18). This one principle, of which all the pages of both the Old and New Testament bear witness, drives away any and all fantasies of the doctrine of perfectibility— the kind of fantasies that allow no belief in original sin and depravity and no desire for regeneration and redemption. Fredrich von Schlegel described this distinction as lying at the heart of the "two main views of history." The one he calls "irreligion," the other "the historic religion."

[71] *Groen: This is also how matters developed with regard to politics. First, an unnatural conception of states was formed. Thereafter this conception was projected onto all states, both ancient and modern, because it was in line with the prejudices and presuppositions. Rousseau, Bernardin St. Pierre, and others proceeded from the idea that human shortcomings are the result of societal interaction and dreamt about an ideal image of humanity outside of society. In chaotic and barbaric hordes they saw an unblemished innocence of the original and natural man. The view of the*

development of the civilized nations have been grossly overestimated. Evil is present, even under the veil of civilization. Everywhere there is sin, and everywhere conscience bears witness to the need for redemption and the feeling of deserved punishment.

Sin, though everywhere present, has never been nor remained on the same level. And there has never been a civilization solely characterized by progress to the exclusion of any decline. Redemptive history bears witness to this fact. How quickly after creation was there a need for a global flood! How speedily after judgment, apostasy from the Jewish people. What a constant reminder, not only of God's grace, but also of increasing depravity has that particular people been through the ages!

World history confirms the lessons of redemptive history: the human tendency toward evil and decline through apostasy. No law or philosophy can halt moral decline, which bursts through these like a flood through a dam wall. Even in the history of Greece and Rome, despite all their glory, it can be shown how, as

---

French sophists often had a lamentable impact upon travelers. Von Kotzebue, for example, described the islands of the South Sea as an earthly paradise with angelic people and lamented that the preaching of the gospel resulted in driving out so-called joy and peace of mind with its seriousness and doctrine: "the happy islands were spoiled." Later, however, it was revealed that human sacrifices were commonplace, that more children were murdered than were raised and that the most gruesome deeds abounded. The population of Tahiti, which Cook estimated to be 200,000, was violently reduced to 160,000 in 1797 and later to a mere 8,000. Clearly, there can be found a petrifying manifestation of moral depravity. The Bible and experience teach that such a nation always remains under the iron yoke of sensuality, except if renewed by the gospel, as is now evidenced in some of these islands.

with most nations, moral decline occurred. Their golden age was not followed by a diamond age but by ages of silver, copper, and iron. This general historical truth is an important witness against human pride and imaginary dreams of the perfectibility of mankind.

On the contrary, far from perfect, humanity would have long ago become completely animalistic had it not been for God, who halted this decline by establishing and maintaining His church—the light of the world and the salt of the earth. This divine intervention is evident from all of history and would, if notice were to be taken thereof, bring an end to the theory of perfectibility. Even the conviction that Europe has its preeminence by virtue of Christianity would nullify the claim that our generation is superior to our ancestors.[72] In the progress and expansion of human knowledge, progeny often add to that which was available to their ancestors. But this surely cannot be viewed as evidence of intellectual or moral superiority. In terms of our aesthetic sentiments and our attachment to that which is truly good, how does this generation compare to those who preceded us? Strength of spirit is certainly no characteristic of our age. Even the Middle Ages can boast with its numerous upstanding and great characters, which tower in comparison to the people of the current age. Some crimes, people claim, are now less common. Perhaps, but others are more common than before. And many rightly argue that, if by virtue of increased carefulness, violence is committed in private and not in public, increased slyness and intrigue are the inevitable results.[73] And a century that produces

---

[72] *Groen: In terms of both our legal system and our moral convictions, the current generation of Europeans are reaping the fruits of their great ancestors.*
[73] *Groen: "It can certainly be questioned whether immorality, if opposed merely by reason, cleverness, and*

virtue by means of selfishness presents itself as harmless by virtue of successfully veiling its immorality. Our age is characterized by a systematic rejection of those true principles that run counter to their envisaged course for humanity.[74]

How then has it happened that a system, which is opposed to both the truths of Scripture and history, has made such immense inroads recently? There was a desire for coherence and unity—a desire that unbelief could not fulfill in any other manner. Furthermore, the idea that humans are inherently good is one that naturally befalls depraved minds, especially those desirous of elevating their own generation above all predecessors. Improvement is merely assumed, even if the standard by which it ought to be measured (man or God) is never even considered. And all that is at odds with this worldview is rejected as stagnation and regress. Thereby all of history is distorted and reduced to arbitrariness. This false system only made inroads because of apostasy from the truths revealed in Scripture and history.

But it is difficult to maintain that the continual decline that marks our age is indeed true progress. As soon as the enchantment with it fades, the entire system collapses. The intense decline of our own age is

---

tricks, creates the kind of condition that is to be preferred above complete chaos." —Ancillon. The condition during the Middle Ages was by no means as unbounded and immoral as it is often presented.

[74] Groen: In this regard I do not call upon Bilderdijk or anyone who can be accused of haughtiness. Rather, I prefer Ancillon, a most talented and highly regarded thinker. His book Ueber den Character und die Fortschritte des jetzigen Zeitallers also shows that he identifies very little that is praise of our own era. Unfavorable judgments, even of the poems and songs of praise of this age, are not at all uncommon nowadays.

undeniable. But many, for whom the effects and outworking of the anti-Christian principles remain a mystery, regard the decline as the effects of civilizational exhaustion. This has become a common view of our time.[75]

The historiography has also, in adulterating with unchristian philosophy, reached new lows. Even deism has become prevalent among historians. Under various forms and names, it has become characterized by complete and utter unbelief. Through godless approaches, the spiritual and even moral world has been reduced to a myth. Fatalism, by which man is seen as a machine and criminality as a virtue, or at least as a necessary consequence of circumstances, has become characteristic of history writing.[76] Furthermore we now

---

[75] Groen advocates for a distinctly covenantal analysis of the society of his own time. This view is also central to the core proposition of his magnum opus, *Unbelief and Revolution*, in which he proposes that the epistemic shift away from Christianity through disobedience to God's Law and ordinances manifests in sociopolitical decline. This is intrinsically tied to Groen's philosophy of history, which can be described as the covenantal-logicist view, and in which the tree-and-the-fruits principle plays a decisive role.

[76] *Groen: In this worldview there are no sins, only miscalculations. One of the most prominent works written with this view is the* Histoire de la Revolution *by Thiers. For example, after the members of the National Convention took their places in the Tuileries, there was a battle between the Girondins and Jacobins between August 10, 1792, and May 31, 1793. The Jacobins came out on top, as the Girondins desired more moderation in the application of the revolutionary ideas. In other words, they did not desire to slaughter and sacrifice tens of thousands of people for the revolutionary idols. Now, who deserves some credit here? Those who desired to limit the atrocities as much as possible for as long as possible? Certainly not, says Thiers. Because these atrocities were necessary for the success of the Revolution. Thiers considers the Girondins to be*

commonly find in history writing a form of pantheism and indifference, which completely blurs the distinction between good and evil, and invalidates the preference for the former—a preference that is inseparably tied to faith in God.[77] Thereby an attempt is made to bring man to a kind of lifeless neutrality, without any strength or vitality, which is actually currently considered by many to be the highest achievement of historiography.[78]

---

shortsighted. His idea of greatness is the act of murder, committed for the revolutionary cause, in cold blood.

[77] *Groen: Those who have no moral compass are constantly hurled to and fro. As the* Evangelische Kirchen-Zeitung *describes it: "Versatility is often the result of the absence of a fixed worldview. Whenever there are no foundations of maxims, there is now law for humanity. It is the versatility of a boatman, who has lost all control over his ship and is blown by the wind to a new destination. This false versatility also manifests itself in the historiography of our time. Actors in history are seen as products of nature rather than as free moral beings. The measure of their achievements is reduced to brute power or mere intellect. Presently the likes of Johan von Muller descend along with the author of the Zend-Avesta in contemplative devotion, and enthusiasm is generated by Epicurean hedonism. In such a view of history all are considered great that are effective and powerful, including Gregory the Great, Frederick the Great, Jesus, and Mohammed. Its presentation of the human spirit is devoid of any existence of truth or lies, and we desire that the true spirit of man not be merely overlooked, and that truth and lies be clearly presented as such, so that man can learn from history. This is also missing from the historiography of the very talented Johann Gottfried Herder."*

[78] *Groen: I do not desire for the writer of history to constantly judge and argue every historical event, and I highly value accurate description of historical reality, but in avoiding every argument and ignoring all cause and effect, the philosophical-historical school completely explains away all the lessons of history.*

Here we witness the same transition in the historiography that we discussed earlier with regard to general principles: in forsaking the Christian faith, we get a diversity of worldviews, arbitrary theories, doubt, and self-deception. The truth, even if exchanged for false ideas by the non-Christian, is not thereby invalidated, and the Christian can rejoice in a holism that false philosophy seeks in vain.[79]

Let us now discuss what history is in light of the gospel. Christianity must be the heart and soul of history. This naturally follows from the nature of the matter and is also proven by experience.

Christ is the Alpha and Omega of the yearbooks of humanity. Holy Scripture contains the plan of God; the intentions of men, slender beings (even if they consider themselves important) can never be considered more than trivial when viewed in light of the God of heaven and earth's eternal design; in fact, our intentions only acquire significance when viewed in relation to the main purpose of this design. This divine plan is set forth clearly in the Bible: the victory of the Kingdom of Christ over him that has been a murderer from the very beginning, and the salvation of those who are, by means of a true faith in their Redeemer, included in this Kingdom. To this plan, all of history is subject.[80]

---

[79] *Groen: There is a unity that corresponds with truth, and one that constantly progresses free from human manipulation and grants unto all historical events their place and significance, as well as strength and life to history as a whole and all its parts—one by which God's design and maintenance for the purpose of the glorification of Christ through His redeemed church becomes visible.*

[80] Groen sees God's redemptive plan for creation as the key to understanding the essence of history, which needs to be understood in terms of both its cosmological genesis in its sovereign divine design, as well as its cosmological telos in the glorification of Christ's Lordship.

Therefore, the heart and soul of all of history should be the history of the Christian Church—that is, the description, not of the history of denominations or sects, but of the continual work of God's Spirit and His revelation for reforming and maintaining His church. Without an emphasis on this one main issue, there can be no true history of the world and no true philosophy of history, no true history of humanity or of civilization, not even a truly pragmatic history, where the deceptive appearances are equated with the essence of the matter.[81] The main themes and purpose of the history of the world are, even to the Christian who has not extensively studied history, no mystery. The Bible, from its account of creation unto the final prophecies of the apostles, where man is being guided into the gates of heaven, has already described to us the course of the ages in the fate of the church. Already the paradise promise itself reveals the unity of history, the outcome of which is the defeat of evil and the condition of which is engagement in battle, with the Seed of the woman being the Victor and Redeemer, who is unchangeable yesterday, today, and unto eternity.

Let us investigate how history itself confirms the truth of revelation. It reveals the perpetual battle for godly truth against unbelief and superstition. It reveals the higher power, by which the church, reawakened and renewed, is able to resist all attacks from without as well as within. God's glory and human depravity time and again come to the fore, and the consequences and outcomes of that contrast offer a shadow and a

---

[81] *Groen: A history of humanity that is at odds with the Bible is an anti-historical novel. A history of civilization, which does not take divine revelation into account, is like a description of fruits without any knowledge of the tree—it is a description of phenomena without any knowledge of their cause or purpose.*

precursor of the government of the world, which is destined to close out the history of the world as we know it.

Think of the world prior to the flood. Pride and immorality prevailed, but the preaching of justice continued even in the midst of all the indifference and mockery, and in the midst of a general extermination, a single believer was made the new progenitor of the human race.

Think of the history prior to Christ where God allowed the pagans to continue to dwell in their own ways in contrast to his elect people. Their path was the way to destruction and led to barbarism. In recognizing all the glory of the Roman and Greek civilizations, we often tend to forget the superstition of many, the hypocrisy of the priests, the godlessness of the higher classes, and the rapidly increasing immorality. It is well-known that the Israelites, a gifted yet highly depraved people, after having been repeatedly seduced into idolatry, were divided by Pharisaism and Sadduceeism as well as doubt and self-righteousness. Darkness and sin were everywhere when Christ, the Light of the world, appeared on earth.

After Christ, it is important to take note of both the pagans as well as the Christian people, who came to replace the Jewish people. Of the former it can be said that they became increasingly bewildered and depraved. With regard to Christianity, it must be said that the development of European civilization is intrinsically related to the spread of Christianity across the continent as well as the impact of the Reformation.

The advance of the gospel effectuates, even in apparent shortage of means, great achievements by virtue of its divine power. Through it, a new world has been formed and the European people have been reborn. What would have become of the wild natural existence of the Germanic and Roman peoples had it not been for this life principle? But Christianity conquered all resistance, and both the Roman and Germanic people knelt before the cross and a decrepit Europe rose with youthful strength. Whereas Europe was previously headed toward disintegration and destruction, the concepts of right, order, and morality now returned to its public life. This rejuvenation of Europe should rightly be regarded as a miracle.[82] If we consider the elements that shaped this renewal of Europe, it is not the remnants of chaos, but rather the return of order, that causes awe.

Let us proceed a few centuries further to when the Reformation lamentably became a necessity, but one that produced glorious fruits. Christianity was now, after the gospel had driven out polytheism and idolatry, plagued by superstition. The Greek empire especially was marked by vain disputes over insignificant issues. In the east, Mohammed injected a false religion into an already syncretistic Christianity. The Greek Church separated itself from Western Christendom. Most of Europe was now suffering the yoke of papal hierarchy, and with the trivialization of the Bible, idolatry returned in the form of prayers to

---

[82] *Groen: Gibbon tries to explain the rise of Christianity without regard to any supernatural forces. However, in his very own argument, it can clearly be seen that even if the world had become prepared for the acceptance of the gospel, the seed of the gospel in Europe would have soon been smothered if the doctrine of Christ had a merely human and not a divine character and if there had been not a more powerful protection for the gospel than mere circumstances. Among the natural causes he mentions, he includes the "virtues of the first Christians." But where did these virtues, which could not have been effectuated by any human philosophy, especially in the midst of such radical moral decline, originate?*

the saints. Christ, by means of the abuse of indulgences, was reduced to a servant of sin. Many died by being burned at the stake when they stood up for their faith and the gospel was persecuted by both the church and secular authorities. But in the midst of all of this Christ's Church was protected and preserved. Before Luther there was Huss, and before Huss there was Wycliffe and before Wycliffe there were many famous, but also many unknown, martyrs. When, with the Reformation, the Bible was once again brought to the fore, a time of unprecedented strength and moral standards started, in which the wholesome influence of the gospel was gloriously evident.

What did our fathers believe and what do we believe? The general blessings of the gospel did not last as long as the wars that resulted from this repentance. The syncretism, temporarily stopped in its tracks, returned to take its normal course. Superstition increasingly established itself in Roman countries, while the Protestant Churches came to be characterized by a dead orthodoxy. Apostasy gradually became prevalent in the sciences and in society in general, even in the church: in the Roman Church veiled by traditional rituals and forms, in the Protestant Church in the form of higher criticism, rationalism, and neology. Whereas before godlessness prevailed in particular among the higher classes, now it has spread to all. The hatred of Christianity has developed into religious apathy and the practical atheism of the eighteenth century has transformed itself into a practical materialism. While lamenting these developments, we must also acknowledge that even in the midst of overwhelming unbelief, the supremacy of faith is revealed and that even now when unbelief seems to be everywhere, the foundation is being laid for a new victory of the Christian faith. The gospel has, after all, outlived all past anti-Christian systems: the uncertainty that characterizes science after forsaking religion amplifies how unmissable the light of Scripture is. And the Christian truth is even now maintained in those places where unbelief had most prominently raised up its most philosophical systems.[83] There are now even signs of revival in those countries where all signs of religiosity seemed to have been wiped out. More people are coming to acknowledge the central truths of the Bible, which the Christian acknowledges to have come from above.

These few examples sufficiently show that the history and fate of Europe are intrinsically tied to the spread, development, restoration, and apostasy of Christianity. And as the hand of the Lord is never absent, our future is also dependent upon the restoration of Christianity. But we must look even further than European Christianity, since also in the field of world history the principles of Christianity can never be overlooked. The Jewish people serve as an example of this, as their reality sheds light upon the very truth they deny. Europe has conquered the false prophet Mohammed and the Turkish empire. We have taken the Bible to the utmost ends of the earth—to the most isolated peoples. While unbelief externally seems to be winning, Satan's inevitable fall is fast approaching, and the return of our Lord, for which we must continue to long, and the great battle between light and darkness are probably not as far off in the distant future as the naive or unbelieving may presume.

While the times may be uncertain, our cause is not. It is with the Church of Christ as it is with every individual Christian. All things work together for our

---

[83] Groen: *Think of Geneva and Berlin.*

good and all events are directed at the glorification and victory of the church. In this world history finds its true meaning. On the other side of the grave, only the history of our spiritual lives matters. Likewise, the history of the world forms the casing of the gospel's development. With regard to the triumphant church, history is the culm by which the seed is braised unto ripeness and the cell in which a beautiful butterfly is formed and, while the world and its glory is passing, this is the sole genuine reason why history is worth investigating.

Part 2: Philosophy and History

Incoherence is inherent to false concepts and false principles, which have sadly become dominant in the sciences. Philosophy is also separated from history. Therefore, I would like to emphasize the relationship between philosophy and history, and thereafter show how this manifests in politics.

The relationship is simple. Philosophy investigates the essence of things, of which history contains the imprint. The philosopher must not attempt to shape, but rather to discover what exists independently of him and his opinions. A false philosophy, on the contrary, proceeds from arbitrary ideas and presuppositions. Just as the true philosopher finds support and confirmation in history, so the sophist, addicted to the inventions of his own mind, would not find in history anything but contradictions.[84]

---

[84] Groen here discards any idea of historiography as a mental construct. This bizarre view would, lamentably, eventually become tremendously popular a century after his death with the rise of postmodernism.

If one were to attempt to isolate oneself from history, one would not be able to defend oneself upon closer investigation. Many claim that philosophy is preoccupied with general or abstract principles, which may be true, even if these haven't been applied in practice. While this may be true, what does it prove? That the seal exists, even before it has been imprinted? Still, the relationship between the seal and its stamp cannot be denied.[85]

Further, some claim that a theory remains true even if it is foolishly resisted in practice. This is undoubtedly true of course, since light remains light even when completely covered and hidden, but those who reject the light itself will always remain in darkness. Thus, those who do not apply true theories in practice would pay the price for their stubbornness, and in this way, even by means of rejection and disregard, a true theory's inherent relationship to practice is confirmed. In accordance with the meaning of the word itself, "practice" is a reflection and expression of the highest essence. As long as practice does not degenerate into arbitrariness, its durability and correspondence to truth is confirmed either by the rejection thereof or adherence thereunto.

Another claim is that philosophy ought to reveal purer and higher truths than history and nature. Who would not deny this? Essence is more complete than shadows and the practical application never fully

---

[85] As before, we find a clear expression of Groen's covenantal-logicist view, in which the connection between theoretical and practical truth is seen as an intrinsic one based on the sovereignty with which divine providence guides the flow of all of history. God has created reality and ordained history in accordance with His will as revealed in Scripture, and therefore revealed truths and experienced reality are perfectly in accord.

corresponds to the theoretical model. The essence is more complete than its shadows. An abstract conceptualization of a principle is more complete than what can be derived from its practical application, but the truth thereof must also be manifested in practice, and the practice itself must confirm whatever is proposed as the theoretical essence of the matter. Philosophical truth is reflected by history and historical truth is rooted in philosophy.

But how is this relationship between philosophy and history represented in politics?

Any political theory that disregards history hides behind the same argument it uses to veil its anti-historical philosophy. It argues that the lessons of history are irrelevant since the ideal is always to be elevated above practical experience. This distinction is to be acknowledged, of course. I do not deny that abstract representations are always purer than practical applications, but I wish to emphasize their intrinsic relationship. We must always take into account the reality of things. An artist who paints a picture of a human being needs to take human nature into account and his representation would by no means be ideal if he were to enforce his own, distorted ideas of what it means to be human upon it. Likewise, I may also advocate political ideals that have not been realized in practice among any nation. But the first principle remains that it must be a practical politics, founded upon reality.

And the systems that have come out of the ever-advancing anti-Christian philosophy do not pass the test of reality. And this is no wonder: this philosophy was always going to descend into idle fantasies. In earlier times, people generally thought about the reality of a matter in terms of nature and history. An artist who desired to paint a beautiful woman based his work on real, existing models. The theory of poetry was formulated by means of the study of existing poetry. The theory of rhetoric was based on studying rhetorical masterpieces. Likewise, in the formulation of a good political theory, the study of historical states is absolutely essential. The new philosophy, which identifies perfection with the mind of the philosopher, imagining that there is no need to be aided by practical experience, brings forth abstractions of the mind that bear no correspondence to the realities of the law, of man, or of the state.

Law itself is founded upon the reality of God.[86] Apostasy results in the forsaking of true law. For atheists, there are only natural impulses, no natural law. There are, of course, the necessary duties that naturally accompany mutual interaction, but in order to maintain right and duty and order, a common law of justice and love, and a Lawgiver that authors and maintains that law, is inescapable. Conscience and ethical feelings are but a bland echo of God's Law, and where this law is forsaken, duty is completely dissolved in pride and selfishness.

---

[86] Groen: *"The so-called 'free-thinkers' and the atheists can claim whatever they like, the reality is that there is no other foundation for human society than the will of God, that is the will which is revealed by his Spirit and is implanted in our hearts. The Holy Spirit is our Lawgiver, and his commands take precedence above all others. All the old philosophers acknowledged this and the most prominent philosophers and jurists of all times did not shy away from seeing that human society is founded upon the will of God."* —Von Haller. *Any science falls apart when it fails to acknowledge the reality of God. Knowledge of proximate causes is void so long as the ultimate cause remains unacknowledged. To attribute independence to secondary causes has been the root of many forms of scientific idolatry.*

The history of the new philosophy evidences exactly what becomes of rights once the highest origins thereof are disregarded. Recourse is taken in an imagined or conventional law: in the arbitrary approval of either one or of many. Not only have human abstractions become the only standard for law, but the very existence of an independent standard has been denied. The very character and essence of law are reduced to the desires of the mob or the majority. The foolish and the antichrist claim that law was invented by mankind for the benefit of society. In this way, the law of nature and politics is buried, and only the interests of the state remain.

In the same way, the essence of human nature is denied. Our relation to God, the first principle of our existence, is completely disregarded.[87] Man is held to be not only inherently good but outstanding. Our weaknesses are not denied, but we are regarded as being able to achieve perfection through participating in civilization itself. The revealed truths regarding the moral depravity of mankind are also disregarded, even by those who confess to be Christians. While there are doctrines that belong to the domain of religion exclusively, because divine revelation is completely true, all theories of natural law that contradict Holy Scripture are to be discarded as false. Objective self-perceptions[88] would have confirmed the true theories

---

[87] *Groen: Cicero writes that "the nature of law must be sought in the nature of man" but also tellingly adds "but this nature was endowed to us by the immortal gods, so that, by means of it we can learn the divine will."*

[88] *Groen: If natural law is based on knowledge of the self, outside of the light of revelation, conceptions of the self would always be distorted in one direction or the other. Then this legal theory, based solely on conceptions of the human mind, is just as incomplete as it is unstable, and, by*

of course, but people were too consumed with foreign ideals to be objective. In the contemporary context, conceptions of natural law most often disregard the central characteristic of human nature itself—namely, depravity.[89]

The builders of the new politics are completely ignorant of the true foundations of the state. Their theories, which are based on their apostasy, have sadly become almost universally accepted. The state becomes a commonwealth, formed by virtue of the unification of free and equal individuals and wherein the execution of authority, based on a supposed and imagined permission, is granted to a government responsible to the people. That this proposition is inconsistent with the essence of the state can be shown in many ways—but for now it is enough to show that at the heart of it lies a conviction regarding the natural equality and liberty of all people, something which is shown to be false by everyday experience.

Since such a political theory cannot be harmonized with history, history has to be either discarded or distorted. Initially, distortion was tried. In history was sought only that which could justify the opinions of its

---

virtue of the fact that it starts from false principles, can only effectuate false conclusions.

[89] Here Groen echoes the Reformed confessional standards. *The Canons of Dort* (1619) III/IV article 4 states: "To be sure, there is left in man after the fall, some light of nature, whereby he retains some notions about God, about natural things, and about the difference between what is honorable and shameful, and shows some regard for virtue and outward order. But so far is he from arriving at the saving knowledge of God and true conversion through this light of nature that he does not even use it properly in natural and civil matters. Rather, whatever this light may be, man wholly pollutes it in various ways and suppresses it by his wickedness. In doing so, he renders himself without excuse before God."

proponents. These unbelievers projected their theories upon events and institutions in ancient history and argued that the gradual deviation from these original theories must be rectified.[90] But the distorted nature of their appcal to history becomes increasingly evident every day, even as they continue to develop their theory in terms of its foundations and conclusions. The mask is thereby removed, and they decide to conveniently do away with all that contradicts their opinions. The judgment of history has declared their views

---

[90] *Groen: They see something in history that in reality wasn't there. Upon the republicanism of the ancients, which emphasized the rights of citizens, the idea of universal human rights is projected. The mighty rule of King Charlemagne was, by virtue of the writing of Mably, Montesquieu, and others, reimagined as a constitutional republic, and the aristocracy reimagined as a convention of the sovereign people. By virtue of this false interpretation, all political arrangements were de-rooted from their original intentions, with only Great Britain maintaining the original principles. But even the English constitution was criticized in as much as it failed to reflect the liberal principles. In various ways, the true lessons of history had to be distorted. Where legitimate authority was historically maintained, it was reduced to tyranny and shameful rebellion was reimagined to be attempted at the re-establishment of true rights. Even unto nations, in their resistance to tyranny, were attributed the kind of ideas that they undoubtedly would have shunned. The doctrinaires of the Enlightenment appealed to the Revolution of 1688 and, blinded by the similarities in form with the French Revolution, denied all the very significant differences in principles. The Swiss radicals imagine themselves to be following in the footsteps of their predecessors, even in advocating the opposite of what their ancestors did. The* Gazette de France *(a newspaper that, in following the zeitgeist, has forsaken the path of truth) projects upon the entire history of France, from the days of the Merovingians, a monarcho-republican form of government.*

deficient.[91] Their false theories lie at the very heart of their distortion of history. A state like the one they propose has no historical precedent. Such a state there never was and never could be. And why not? Not because historical states fell short of the ideal, but because their very ideal amounts to a distortion of reality that cannot exist in reality. Their political theory was not simply never historically applied but it is in reality inapplicable altogether. But despite all this, their conceit continues.[92] That which is contrary to nature is proposed as ideal, and the highest perfection is sought in greatly distorted theories.[93] As their

---

[91] Groen: With Plato, the historical principle, even in his work de Republica, is never completely ignored. With Aristotle, in his detailed description of the 255 commonwealths that were foundational to his very argument, and Cicero, when portraying his ideals for the Roman political order, true knowledge of history was regarded as integral to all political theorizations. Hugo Grotius, to whom liberals love to appeal, would also have rejected their sharp distinction between experience and theory.

[92] Groen: It is true that in politics, the ideal state must be envisaged, but this ideal, in order to be pure, must always be in accordance with reality.

[93] Groen: "The universal law which extends itself to all states would vary in every particular application" —Boehmer. "What today is considered a universal philosophy nowhere exists, is nowhere applicable, and is necessarily inapplicable" —Von Haller. Von Haller has, in many places, beautifully explained the relationship between philosophy and history in terms of its application to politics. Yet many in the Netherlands have condemned him without even reading his work. By not reading that which you disapprove of, the art of critical thinking is greatly diminished. The prejudice against Von Haller, reflected in the fact that he is regarded, in spite of his advocacy for the true rights of nations, as a proponent of despotism, has sadly been strengthened by his conversion to Roman

philosophy teaches the state must be, so they argue, even if all experience teaches us lessons to the contrary.[94] And so whatever does not correspond to this false philosophy is considered to be injustice and oppression and therefore worthless. Therefore, because every historical state and commonwealth is in some way a reflection of the true essence of politics, no historical state can escape their condemnation. What an absurd pretension of philosophical excellence!

Catholicism. Although his move toward Roman Catholicism and away from Protestantism is lamentable, we should not be swept away by the false accusations of his opponents. Even though his Catholicism is evident in his writings, the core of his theory, by which he dismantles liberal heresies, is in no way directly dependent upon Roman Catholic doctrines. In the midst of misrepresentations, professor Star Numan has been an exception in his fair analysis of Von Haller, by writing in his exemplary Treatise de Principe Machiavelli *that "the manner in which the royal governments in many parts of Europe originated from the customs and institutions of the Germans and the nature of these governments is nowhere more keenly described than in the works of Von Haller." And this is only one of the many great aspects of Von Haller's contribution to political theory. By proving that there is no tension between human nature and politics and that states are the organic and not artificial products of historical development, he has, by virtue of one central truth, refuted a thousand lies.*

[94] *Groen: The political system of a state can change, but not its essence. Ancillon writes that "the state is a fact." This fact, confirmed by a thousand historical experiences, was not considered to be an obstacle to idiosyncrasy. Rousseau's social contract theory, for example, simply ignores this reality. False presuppositions regarding the origin of states will never lead to clarification of the nature thereof. While it may be at times valuable to, in the process of philosophical speculation, place oneself outside the confines of history, whenever one knows that the theory is disproved by reality itself, one can really simply spare oneself the effort of developing that false theory.*

What would we make of a psychology or a physiology that describes humans with characteristics and limbs we do not truly possess? What then should we think of a philosopher who, when shown that all reality contradicts his theory, simply responds that humans aren't supposed to be this way or even that they are not really humans if they do not fit his abstract conceptualization of humanity? Just like our anthropology must apply to humanity, so our politics must be applicable to statehood.[95] True politics are confirmed by history. Experience confirms axioms and warns us when theories deviate from truth. Experience is the test of the truth or falsehood of any theory.[96] The modern politics regard all states as essentially the same. They supposedly all exhibit the same characteristics. And yet some, disillusioned by the modern theory, have come to regard theory as subservient to the historical development of each state, thereby denying the existence of any political theory whatsoever.

---

[95] Groen: "A mathematician does not claim to have seen all the triangles in the world in order to describe the principles of trigonometry, since these characteristics apply to all triangles without exception. That which is derived from the nature of the triangle itself is necessarily applicable to all the world's triangles, even in their diversity" —Von Haller.

[96] Groen: "General politics or rather the history of the natural development of states is not only derived from experience, as this is in no way comprehensive to show the universality and inescapability of the matter—at least not independent of an idea regarding the true nature of the state, which, even if its criteria and truth was acquirable by reason, needs to be confirmed by experience in terms of its effects and consequences, which would show it to be truly organic. Experience is the true confirmation of the reasonable criteria, which by itself is certainly not the source of truth" —Von Haller.

Just like there can be no political philosophy that is consequently disproven by experience, there is no historical affirmation of a false political philosophy. Historical affirmation is the inevitable consequence of the application of true principles to political theory. There is no imprint possible without a seal, no coin without a coinage, and the view of any particular is dependent upon the whole to which it belongs. Inasmuch as those who advocate for a historical politics mean to do away with false theories, they are right, but they must still carefully go about identifying the true imprint of true principles upon history.

The true political theory is simple, and long explanations are much more necessary in refuting false theories than in expounding the truth.[97] The necessity of doing polemics has multiplied the workload of the political theorists of our day tenfold. The walls and chains, which hinder the pure light of truth from being revealed to us, need to be removed. And once this has been accomplished, there is no need for an elaborate explanation of the essence and strength of this light. And yet, the simplicity of the true political theory is no reason to cast doubt regarding it. Rather, the simplicity itself should serve as a seal of its truth.

In addition to the reality of a universally true political theory, we must also acknowledge the particularity of the application thereof to the life of a particular nation. In the national life of a particular people, political theory finds its application.[98] Thus it

---

[97] *Groen: According to Von Haller, politics is the application of the general divine law of justice and love to the essence of states, so that political theory, in all of its aspects and applications, could also be appropriately called "the theory of social conditions, as it encompasses all of these."*

[98] *Groen: What Von Haller writes regarding the Swiss people is also applicable to other nations: "Firstly we seek*

is founded upon both history and philosophy—that is, the aggregation of historical rights as the particular manifestation of a universal theory.[99]

As soon as the revolutionary or anti-Christian political theory has been accepted, then the philosophical element of political theory comes into inevitable conflict with the historical element thereof. And why is this? Not because the new political theory claims that the particular application of political theory should be in accordance with the universal principles thereof—because in this regard it is absolutely right— but because the application of its universal principles to the particular is impossible since they deny the very essence and nature of both peoples and states. This is why it rejects all particularities. But with unshakable firmness, they accuse all those who oppose their ideas of prejudice and misunderstanding. In this regard, they even argue that the stronger the resistance to their ideas is, the more necessary its application becomes and that all which contradicts its theories cannot be regarded as a true national life, since through the application of its theories the true yet suppressed natural life emerges. They don't realize that any constitution that is based solely on abstractions can only be arbitrary, unnatural, and anti-national. In this regard their anti-historical philosophical politics is by

---

to understand the true facts of the matter, after which we seek to apply it with wisdom to our particular legal and political context."

[99] *Groen: In the consistent application of Roman law, everyone everywhere sees the life and work of true principles. Therefore, it is with good reason commonly referred to as "natural law personified," and this must be true to every particular application of legal principles to a people's national life.*

its very nature anti-national—that is, opposed to historically acquired rights.[100]

On the contrary, whenever the historical principle is derived from true philosophy—that is, the true essence of reality—it needn't be forced upon a people because it is already integrally present in every state. It can be identified in the history of every particular nation, as the particular political application can be observed in the national life of every people—just like every individual, while being part of a universal humanity, has their own unique characteristics and physiognomy. In such a political theory the central motto is "maintain and improve" not "destroy and recreate." The present should always be the development of the past.

A written constitution can certainly be harmonized with true political practice, inasmuch as it amounts to the putting to paper of that which is prescribed by the natural inclinations of the relevant people and state.[101]

---

[100] Here again Groen expresses the principle of the One-and-the-Many—that is, of universality and particularity, which stand in opposition with one another in non-Christian philosophies but is resolved in the biblical worldview wherein neither the universal nor the particular aspects of humanity are recognized as ultimate, but rather as a perfect, harmonious reflection of the *imago Dei*, of mankind being created in the image of the one God who created man "in *our* image, after *our* likeness" (Genesis 1:26—plurality emphasized). That is, mankind is created in the image and likeness of the Triune God, who is both three persons yet one God.

[101] *Groen: The forceful implementation of the propositions of a false philosophy, also in common law, has been one of the greatest tragedies ever to befall Europe. Naturally the composition of constitutions and written laws are not disagreeable in themselves, but the lawgiver and politician should always follow this simple rule: write the law as it is and not as I desire it to be.*

A true constitution is the charter in which the result of national history is documented and should in no way be the machine by which the state is formed or the garb by which the nation is contorted.[102] Such a political practice, even when it has become common, can only defend itself by means of violence, since it vehemently suppresses and fails to appreciate the true nature of humanity. In nature and in law, all that is particular

---

(cont.) *Written constitutions, inasmuch as they are the products of false theories, therefore need not be wholly discarded but need to be informed with a different spirit and consequently also revised. Upon these products of false philosophy, true philosophy needs to be imprinted. Then these theoretical documents will also become truly historical.*

[102] *Groen: Such a constitution is the description of the natural character in which the life of a nation manifests itself. This character develops in accordance with the people and the dynasty from which the state originated. Cato rightly observes: "No particular time nor any particular generation ought to be the foundation of the republic." The spirit of the nation is revealed in its citizenry. State and fatherland and nation ought to be harmonized, and where this is not done, politics are not built upon sure foundations. Upon nations who, through artificial constitutions are recreated in a state, the words of Herder are applicable: "A nation is both a product of nature as well as a family, only one with many branches. Nothing seems quite so contrary to the purpose of government as the wild intermixing of races and nations under one scepter. In this way incompatible parts are glued together in a flimsy machine, called the machine of the state, without an inherent harmonious life of or sympathy between the parts. Empires such as these make it impossible for even the best monarchs to govern as the father of the fatherland." What is here said, unjustly, regarding submission to the same scepter, is certainly applicable to the assimilation of nations under one liberal constitution. (And the Netherlands has already experienced this!)*

and just remains unappreciated by any political theory that denies historical realities.

And yet, this arbitrary political theory and practice has now become commonplace. This lamentable truth is now well-known, but it is certainly nothing to become excited about. In order to counter the unity of philosophy, history, and revelation, the new philosophy had to be simultaneously anti-historical and anti-Christian. By virtue of its forceful application, an anti-Christian and anti-historical practice was developed, in which the essence of true law and philosophy was sacrificed. It is because of this inevitable conflict between nature and unnatural compulsion that Europe is currently experiencing such constant unrest and agony. A philosophy that has occupied itself with fantasies far removed from reality has experimented with the complete destruction of everything it touches. This has, of course, been shown to be unachievable because of the fact that the realities of nature are indestructible. This philosophy's systematic wrath was able to de-root, but not to completely cut off.[103] Existing states could not be

---

[103] *Groen: It is in light of these realities that the revision of the Dutch constitution must also be completed. Yet some still desire a liberal revision—that is, the development of false principles, by which they are still charmed, even after all their failures. Others (and these currently make up the majority) currently fear such a revision and with good reason. Perhaps there are also those who desire to see the constitution abolished altogether and the situation in the Netherlands restored to what it had been prior to 1795. Of these people one need not even be mindful since they are very few in number and there is no strength in their position. The desire to ignore forty years of development is an anti-historical position in itself. Even if the revolutionary principle is to be discarded, the acquired rights of the past forty years are to be respected. But what is it then that the*

completely overthrown, and no state could be formed on the basis of its principles. The impotence of the new philosophy is itself a testimony to the unity between philosophy and history.

Dutch constitution needs? Not a liberal revision, not a revision in form only and also no abolishment, but rather maintenance and improvement in the Christian-historical sense. Then the Bible would again be the highest standard, and no law would be dependent upon the arbitrary will of a constitutional assembly.

If a constitution has been authored in the same liberal spirit that prevailed in most European countries after the fall of Napoleon, then revision becomes necessary. Subjection, even unto that which one does not approve of, is often the duty of the Christian. Yet a political system based upon the rejection of the gospel would eventually make the active participation of the Christian a practical impossibility, with the irony being that Christians who remain loyal to true doctrines would become political pariahs in a country that was historically shaped by the Protestant Church.

5
General Agreement

More often than not there is either too little or too much value attached to the opinions of others. Allow me in this regard to explain firstly the value of general agreement, thereafter public opinion, and finally the judgment of competent judges.

What do we understand by "general agreement?" In our context, it is amazing how many different opinions and views there are, but there still remain certain truths among which there has been agreement among all people in all ages. There are many things that all people disapprove of, and some that are undoubtedly believed by all, and much that all regard as false. Furthermore, there are certain duties about which everyone agrees and certain crimes that all hold as such. A few exceptions exist, of course, but this does not negate the general agreement of thought regarding morals and practice present among all nations of all times, which form the opinions not of the day but of humanity in general.

The value of this agreement cannot be overlooked. The motto *vox populi, vox Dei*, understood in light of this common agreement, has some truth to it. But it became blasphemous once it came to entail the elevation of the views of the people above the Law of God. Nonetheless, it can be appreciated inasmuch as it refers to the voice of God as echoed in human nature that, in spite of human nature's slavery unto sin, has still preserved some of the original goodness and in which some part of the will of our heavenly Lawgiver has still remained. The agreement of all, while not the cause or foundation of truth, is in some sense a characteristic of truth.[104] Truth, shining like light in the darkness, has been imprinted on the hearts and minds of humanity.[105] It is also to be sought in this imprint and is therefore not normally to be found in that which is wholly new and unprecedented.

But what about instances where general agreement is at odds with true principles? The answer must be clear. For the truth everything must be heeded, and the highest truth can be found in proven principles. Nonetheless, it would most often be shown that in such cases people either propose something as a common agreement that in reality is not or they are misled and blinded by false principles.

---

[104] *Groen:* "Semper, ubique, ad omnius: 'Always, everywhere and to all'—the unmistakable character of truth and its divine origin. This was also confirmed by Cicero: 'Universal consensus is the voice of nature'. Not as if it was designed by humanity, as proposed by the new philosophy, but rather it reflects truths inherent to humanity as created reality." This sentiment was also echoed in France by De Bonald and de Lamennais.*

[105] Here Groen echoes the thoughts of the great Federalist thinker Johannes Althusius (1563–1638), who argued that man, by virtue of being created in the image of God, is endowed with an innate knowledge of God's will, which is morally useful inasmuch as it inclines one to the Decalogue (Johannes Althusius, *Politica*, [Groningen: Johannes Radeus, 1610], 118).

It is advisable that, when the agreement of not only your peers (since every generation has been misled by some form of heresy) but those of all ages are against you, you should not be overconfident in your opinion. It would be best not to simply discard that which has always been held by all but to rather investigate and reconsider it thoroughly. If this had been done in this age of false philosophy, then the arbitrary opinions of the day would not have been so much more highly regarded than the agreement of the ages, and the judgments of history would not have been so hastily clamored down.

What we have said regarding general agreement clearly differentiates it from what is known as "public opinion."

Public opinion is one of those dangerous terms that is currently commonly in use and exhibits an unbelievable elasticity in terms of its meaning. There is almost nothing now that does not claim this title— including the opinion of an entire nation and a single city, an opinion that has been held for ages, and also one that disappears within a couple of days from rearing its head. But the word itself has no dubious meaning, and the grammatical analysis thereof offers us no arbitrary explanation, albeit one that is often ignored. Public opinion, because of the firmly held conviction regarding its truth, often exhibits the character of a general heresy because it remains effectively immune to criticism and thorough investigation and therefore effectively most often becomes a mere publicly held prejudice.

Public opinion is almost always formed prematurely, with self-interest and emotions playing the greatest role in shaping it. And because it is never subjected to the light of principles nor the scrutiny of brave and wise men, it is highly susceptible to be swept along with the false ideas of heretics. It is not possible to acknowledge public opinion, the tendency toward error that is confirmed daily, as any kind of standard. Even if public opinion is in rare cases worthy of being honored, it is most often contemptible. Nonetheless, its power can never be underestimated. Opinions effectuate actions, after all. Public opinion is a mighty lever, a power unto which we cannot afford to be indifferent. Even the physician takes the emotional state of his patient into account. The state must of course never be blown to and fro by public opinion but must always be aware of it and take it into consideration—just like the boatman, in steering his ship, knows how to make the best use of the way the wind blows. This comparison, while useful, is with regard to one very important aspect not truly applicable. While the forces of nature may be completely beyond our control in the sense that we can truly do nothing about them, public opinion can be shaped. But wherein lies the strength to do this? In the natural power of principles. Where the principles are solid, one need not fear public opinion.[106] Not in

---

[106] *Groen: It is, after all, in the strength of the prevalent principles that the seeming omnipotence of public opinion lies. The latter always stands in direct relation to the former. Opinion is now most often shaped by the press, and sometimes even by only a handful of journalists and plotters. This has been taught to us by the recent history of the fatherland, especially during the years 1828–1830. But what happened here was that it was the journalists, in fact, who instigated the flame of the Belgian Revolution, who drove and steered public opinion in the revolutionary direction. False theories always form the foundation of false opinions. If the rulers of Europe had been more aware of the dangers of the revolutionary theories, they would have paid a lot more attention to what is taught from the pulpits, at the schools, and what the newspapers propagated. They*

suppressing or ignoring it, and neither in attempting to replace it with an artificial opinion, but by proclaiming the truth clearly and by vehemently promoting it among the public. Hereby public opinion would be submitted to legitimate authority, thereby becoming immune to pretension and heresy, and we would gain the upper hand over it even without arbitrarily suppressing it.

Public opinion is today even more dangerous than it has been in times past. People are generally less equipped against it than they were before, despite the fact that it has in turn increased in power. This is due to the general decline in principles along with the popularization of [secular] science and the ease by which information can be propagated nowadays to a very wide audience.

Opinions, in earlier days, were maintained within the bounds of principles, and public opinion itself was limited within the bounds of the Christian religion and Christian ethics. The godless philosophy has, by means of absolving all boundaries, created a kind of public opinion to which principles themselves have become subject, while in reality there are foundational principles that should always remain above scrutiny by public opinion. Truths and principles that were previously acknowledged to be above scrutiny are now simply arbitrarily denied. The terrain of opinions, which was previously understood as not able to impact upon general truths, now apparently has no limits. And now, as the impact of God's Law upon society declines,

---

would have, in order to defeat the revolution, sharply distinguished their own positions from that of the revolutionaries. They would not have regarded material wellbeing as the supposed guarantee against what was essentially a spiritual decay.

more and more authority is attributed to the opinions of fallible people.[107]

Previously science was considered to be the domain of learned men. In general their contributions were broadly appreciated, but public opinion did not function as a court of approval. In this regard, *judicium per pares*—that is, peer-review—was regarded as the standard of approval for scientific contributions. In science, of course, knowledge, not opinions, is what is required. There was a lot about which the general public was not equipped to express opinions. Now the sciences have been popularized and having even a little knowledge is all that is now required to consider oneself an expert. For many, true knowledge of principles and essences has become redundant.[108] No one who has read a few encyclopedias and abstracts can consider themselves to be experts worthy of expressing an expert opinion.

When the nations were much more secluded and national differences were not yet so greatly subdued by commerce and interaction, there were vast differences between thoughts and opinions in accordance with the vast differences in circumstances and character. This has been diminished by means of this mutual interaction, and now there are increasing signs of the development of a general European public opinion.[109]

---

[107] Groen: *The fear of God is the only guarantee against the fear of man.*

[108] Groen: *Competence without character, zeal without knowledge, is useless. Politicians who, lacking true scientific knowledge, were ill-equipped to protect the people against false theories and have caused Europe much suffering.*

[109] Groen: *Most of the European nations have had commonalities since at least the beginning of the Middle Ages, but they have always remained different and distinct in terms of their language, morals, and forms of government. The dominance of the French language and its*

Those who have maintained the arsenal of true principles see this for the monstrosity it is. We should especially pay attention to the meaning of the word "public." The so-called "European opinion" is thankfully not yet the opinion of all.[110] In fact, it is often widely resisted and supported only by a few, yet it presents itself with such great confidence as the public that it is not uncommon for the opinions of a small minority to be presented as the opinions of the general public. By means of the unified message of the journalists, it is able to present itself as such and even to increase its adherence—and while it is propagated everywhere, fewer and fewer people have the courage to openly resist it.

Never in the past has there been such overwhelming propaganda. We live in the century of societies, assemblies, magazines, and newspapers, by which all that is supposed to make up public opinion is outlined to the finest detail. Yet, even while this is

---

literature, and the consequent increased unification, has erased so much that would have been better preserved. The free and fast distribution of propaganda and information is certainly one of the reasons why the national differences have now already been weakened for quite some time. However, the main reason why many of these differences have seemingly disappeared, particularly in the last century, and particularly among the higher classes, can be attributed to the prevalence of a theory that has sought to undermine national distinctions and build a society based on abstractions, thereby effectuating a characterlessness among both individuals and nations.

[110] *Groen: I grant that this opinion now finds its roots in the prevalent mood of the European people, but it was built on the foundation of false principles. This is the only explanation for the triumph of such a small minority during the French Revolution, for example. Even their terror was openly tolerated by the time the public opinion was shaped in accordance with their actions.*

highly lamentable, we must never forget that truth is never dependent upon the destruction of the material means of the enemy. The banning of associations and the limitation of press freedom are characteristic policies of a political position that lacks the correct understanding of the rights, duties, and limitations of government. The more a government lacks strength in principles, the more use it makes of violent and forceful measures.[111] The constant complaints regarding the very existence of societies and newspapers are completely unfounded and ridiculous, much like a dog biting at a stone.[112] The heart of the evil lies not in the manifestation of the theories but in the theories themselves. Wherever they exist, their spread cannot be stopped by political measures as they tend to find a way past all obstacles. The printing press itself is merely a funnel for ideas. Yet it is not the funnel itself that is dangerous but rather the ideas. However, even

---

[111] *Groen: This has been evident throughout the entire revolutionary period, and especially everything we have experienced in Belgium and the Netherlands since 1830. In France they now govern, if one could call it governing, with police, despotic laws, bayonets, and violence. Everywhere where functional atheism has become the foundation of the state and the standard of politics, increased government measures are required—eventually to the point of becoming wholly tyrannical, and even then such a system lacks sufficient strength to maintain itself. Such oppression is certainly not the solution to the spiritual illness currently plaguing society. The current rule by revolutionary theories, through which this societal disease has spread, will simply continue as long as the sovereignty of Christian principles is not re-established. Christianity alone is able to effectively resist liberal theories.*

[112] *Groen: Evil is merely driven deeper into the soul of the nation whenever the external manifestations thereof are banned. The methods of Hippocrates and Boerhaave could certainly teach liberal politicians quite a lot.*

in acknowledging that it would be unwise to counter heresies by means of tyrannical measures, and even given the fact that the current evil cannot be attributed to the media by which it is propagated, it still cannot be denied that the ease with which this propaganda currently takes place has greatly contributed to the contemporary prevalence of false theories. Public opinion came to be perceived as central to societal arrangements once true principles were left behind. Truth, in fact, became dependent upon the assent of the people. Now, whenever there exists a difference in opinion, there remains no standard but the majority of votes. Upon this shaky foundation, conventional truth is founded. Public opinion now has many means to ensure that it is maintained, such as the use of violence, bribery, or assassination—means it liberally makes use of. But in order to do this, of course, public opinion needs a large number of adherents among the people— adherents it has converted by means of its widespread propaganda.

Public opinion would actually have to be shaped by society's wisest and most-equipped men. Sadly, during our own time, public opinion has effectively placed itself above the scrutiny of such men. Whenever any opinion not in accordance with the false revolutionary theories is expressed, it is simply shunned as prejudice and fanaticism.[113]

In every scientific investigation, it remains of utmost importance to keep in mind the sentiments of predecessors who, by virtue of their wisdom and knowledge, have excelled in this particular field. You should never limit yourself to the sentiments prevalent

---

[113] This rhetorical tactic is still commonly employed by leftist revolutionaries in our own day. Think of how those who refuse to fall in line with their agenda are made out to be racists, sexists, homophobes, or fascists.

in your own lifetime. In the sciences, there also exists a hierarchy of experts, and the position of a scholar in the rankings is, for good reason, most often determined by progeny. Therefore, the scientific positions of predecessors ought to enjoy some degree of precedence. The errors that mislead us most often have the same effect on our peers, while our ancestors lived in a radically different atmosphere and could see certain truths more clearly than we can. On the other hand, we, living in a different context, would be less impaired by the errors of previous generations, and there can of course always be redundancies and errors in the quotes of predecessors. Nonetheless, the witness of predecessors is most valuable in terms of warning us against errors and establishing the truth. When positioning oneself, it is naturally vital to take into account the witness of many generations as opposed to merely the spirit of the current age, which has most often manifested the most depraved fruits. The principle of *nemini me mancipavi*[114]—that is, not being a slave of anyone's opinion—has in our contemporary age come to mean "I believe only in myself, and even if I have no knowledge of the matter, I still refuse to listen to those who have spent a lifetime investigating it." Therefore, in being a slave to no one but oneself, man, in desiring to be his own master, actually descends into the vilest form of slavery.

Revelation, philosophy, history, and general agreement are the foundations of science. They are not of equal value, however, even if they all share a single source. Because they share a single source, however, they are almost always harmonious. However, whenever apparent conflicts between these

---

[114] The Latin phrase literally means "not selling oneself to anyone."

foundations exist, the revelation of the Bible is to be considered definitive and final. After all, no truth can ever be at odds with the Word of Him who is the Truth, the Way and the Life.

Index

A

Acts 4:19 .... 67n41
Acts 15:22 .... 55n29
Adolphus, Gustavus
.... 86n66
Afgescheidenen
Dutch Conservatives
........................*xvi*n3
Althusius, Johannes
.... 118n105
Ancillon .. 92n74, 109n93
Anglican Church ... 85n66
Anselm of Canterbury
...........................79n57
anti-Christian principles
...................................93
anti-revolutionary ....*ix*,
*xvi*n1, 41, 54n27, 58n32
anti-revolutionary theory
.... 30n6, 54n27
apostasy.........30, 99, 104
Apostolic-Catholic
Church......................55
Aristotle................108n91

B

Arius.............................64
Asia.........................85n66
atheism........... 30, 51, 63,
84n65, 99, 124n111
Augustine 61n35
Austria......................... 67

Bavinck, Herman...63n37
Belgian Revolution of
1830 ......37n14, 39n16,
58n33, 120n106
Belgic Confession
Art. 27 ....48n22
Art. 36 ....52n26
Belgium..........39, 58n33,
124n111
Berlin....................100n83
Bernard of Clairvaux
.... 61n35
Bible.............. *ix*, *x*, *xi*, 42,
49n24, 50, 51, 52n26,
54, 56, 60, 64, 66, 87,

88n69, 90n71, 95,
96n81, 98, 100,
116n103, 127
infallibility of..........62
Bilderdijk........59n34, 61,
92n74
Boehmer............ 108n93
Boerhaave, Herman
........................124n112
Bonaparte, Napoleon
.... 116n103
Borger, E.A. 70n44
Bossuet, Jacques-
Bénigne 64n39
Burke, Edmond 61n36

C

Calvin, John....54, 61n35,
64
Calvinists 64
The Canons of Dort
........................106n89
Catholicism.....55, 56, 63,
67n42, 109n93
Cato 114n102
Charlemagne 107n90
Charles X
of France 1824-1830
.... 37n14
Christendom..........55, 75
Western.................98
Christian Church...30,
47, 48, 60, 65, 96
Christian Historicism
.... 49n23
Christian principles ...*xiv*,
45, 124n111
Christian worldview ... 44
Christianity......34, 37n14,
39, 42, 43n20, 44, 47,
48, 51, 52n25, 53, 54,
67n31, 68, 69n42, 70,

72, 74n51, 78n55,
79n56, 80n59, 81n61,
82, 83, 85n66, 86n66,
88, 91, 93n75, 95, 97,
98n82, 99, 100,
124n111
Church of Rome .... *See*
Roman Catholic
Church
Cicero 38n15, 52n25,
72n48, 75n52, 105n87,
108n91, 118n104
Clark, Gordon.....*xxviii*n4
Claudian...............84n65
Clement of Alexandria
.... 74n51
Colossians 2:3 .... 78n55
Cook, James 90n71
core principles......... *xxvii*
Council of Trent 56
Cyprian................ 61n35

D

De Bonald, Louis
......................118n104
de Lamennais, Félicité
......................118n104
deism......... 48, 51, 86, 93
deist......................68, 86
divine revelation .... *x*, 44,
47, 49n24, 52n25, 68,
84n65, 96n81, 105
doctrine of unbelief.....61,
63
Dutch Catholics.....62n36
Dutch constitution
.... 115n103
Dutch Ideas
magazine................ *xv*
Dutch Protestant Church
......................62n36

Dutch Reformed Church
...................*xvi*n3
Dutch Resistance...86n66

E

Egypt 75n52
empiricism............76n54
England.....61n36, 63, 66,
    67
Enlightenment...*ix*, 30n6,
    54n27, 71n47, 76n54,
    107n90
Ephesians 2:12...... 52n26
Ephesians 4:22, 24
    .... 88n69
epicureanism...............78
epistemological
    rationalism........76n54
epistemology .... *ix*, *x*,
    *xxvii*n4
Erasmus, Desiderius....56
ethics 47n21, 74n52
Christian................ 121
Europe...................33n9,
    35, 53n26, 65, 85n66,
    91, 98n82, 100,
    109n93, 113n101, 115,
    120n106, 122n108
European civilization
    ....32n7, 54, 97
*Evangelische Kirchen-
    Zeitung* .78n55, 81n62,
    88n69, 94n77

F

fatalism.....79n56, 84n65,
    93
fetishism.................... 50
Fichte, Johann Gottlieb
    .... 70n44
first principles ..*xxvii*, 29,
    52

France...33n9, 34n10, 35,
    36, 37, 40n17, 63, 67,
    81n62, 107, 118n104,
    124n111
Frederick the Great ....
    94n77
French Revolution ...... *ix*,
    34n10, 35n11, 54n27,
    107n90, 123n110

G

Gazette de France
    ....107n90
Geneva 100n83
Gibbon, Edward ... 98n82
Girondins 93n76
gospel *xiv*, 39, 43, 44, 45,
    52, 54, 56, 57, 65, 67,
    68, 73, 74, 75, 76, 78,
    81, 83, 84, 85, 86, 88,
    90, 95, 97, 98, 99, 101,
    116
Great Britain 107n90
Greece 75n54, 90
Greek Church 98
Greek civilization 97
Greek empire..............98
Greeks 73, 74n52, 80n59,
    83
Gregory the Great...94n77
Grotius, Hugo...... 108n91
Guido de Bres........ 61n35
Göschel, Carl Friedrich
    .... 78n55

H

Hallam, Henry 85n66
Heeren, Arnold Hermann
    Ludwig.............75n53,
    80n59, 85n66

Herder, Johann Gottfried
.... 94n78, 114n102
Herodotus............. 84n64
Hinduism..................... 51
Hippocrates.........124n112
historiography......93, 94,
95n77, 101n84
Historische Schule..........
49n23, 73n50
Hofstede de Groot..61n35
Holland...................... 38
Holy Scripture.......*xxviii*,
49n24, 62, 69n24, 72,
79n56, 95, 105
Holy Spirit.............79n57,
88n69, 104n86
Homer.................. 84n64
House of Orange
.... 41n18
Huss, John............ 64, 99

I

inalienable rights.........34
Industrial Revolution
.... 30n6
international law.......*xvi*,
xxviii, 34, 40, 47n21,
70, 83
international law.........47
international law.........52
Islam..................... 48, 51
Israelites...............48, 97
Italy 67

J

Jacobins............... 93n76
Jesuits.................... 37n14
Jesus.....................94n77
John 3:3............... 88n69
justice...34, 39, 40n17,
97, 104, 111n97

K

Kant, Immanuel.. 43n20,
76n54
Kuyper, Abraham.. 63n37

L

law...94n77, 104, 105n87,
108n93, 113n101, 114,
116n103, 124n111
Le Maistre, Joseph 74n51
liberal protestants.......62
liberalism .... *ix*, 37
political 57n31
theological..........*xvi*n3
Locke, John........*xxviii*n4
Louis XVIII
of France 1814-1824
.... 37n14
Luke 12:20................. *xix*
Luther, Martin 54, 61n35,
64, 67n41, 79n56, 99
Lutheran church ... 57n31
Lutherans.................. 64

M

Mably, Gabriel Bonnot
.......................107n90
Machiavelli..........109n93
materialism 35, 77, 99
Melanchthon, Philip
.... 61n35
Merovingians 107n90
Middle Ages 57n31, 91,
92n31, 122n109
Mohammed.....51, 94n77,
98, 100
Montesquieu, Charles
.......................107n90
Moses 49n24, 75n52
mysticism..............68, 69,
70n44

N

National Reformed
  Church.................*xvin3*
natural law....49n23, 104,
  105n88, 112n99
Neology.......... 54, 54n28,
  57n31, 59
neo-propositional state.
 32
Netherlands....*xi, xiv*, 34,
  36, 37, 37n14, 39, 40,
  58n33, 66, 67n42,
  70n44, 108n93,
  114n102, 115n103,
  124n111
Numan, Cornelis Star
  .... 109n93

P

paganism 81
papism.........................55
pelagianism 79n56
1 Peter 2:13 .... 67n41
1 Peter 5:1-4 .... 55n29
Philippians 2:13.....79n56
philosophy.............30,
  30n5, 52n25, 59n34,
  68, 70n44, 71, 75,
  78n55, 108n94, 115,
  113n101, 118n104
  anti-Christian... 76, 81,
    103
  atheistic.............60, 63
  Christian political....81
  Greek.....73, 74n51, 75,
    87n68
  pagan......................74
  political.......68n43, 111
  Western.......68, 87n68
Pindar................... 84n64
Plato....38n15, 42, 52n25,
  71n47, 74n51, 108n91

pluralism.............. 63n37
Plutarch................52n25

Politica
  book by Johannes
    Althusius....118n105
political theory ...*x, xi*, 57,
  70, 75n52, 76n54, 103,
  104, 106, 109n93,
  111n97, 112, 113, 115
postmodernism... 101n84
Prince William of Orange
  .... 86n66
Protestant(s) .. 43, 47, 53,
  54, 55, 55, 56, 61n36,
  63n38, 67n42, 85n66
Protestant Church 54, 59,
  62, 64, 66, 99, 116
Protestant Churches...39,
  53, 56, 99
Protestant Confessions...
  61n35, 64n39
Protestant Reformation
  43, 47, 48, 53, 54, 55,
  56, 60, 63, 66, 67, 75,
  80, 97, 98, 99
Protestantism.......53, 54,
  55, 56, 57, 58, 59, 61,
  63, 64, 65, 66, 67, 109
  neo...........................58
providence................... *x*
Psalm 90:10 .... *xix*
public opinion ..*xviii*, 117,
  119, 120n106, 121, 122,
  123n110, 125

R

rationalism 54, 57, 68, 69
rationalist theology
  ....54n28, 59, 69
regeneration............... 65

Revolution of 1688
  67n42, 85n66, 107n90
Revolution of 1830
  Second French.........34
revolutionary theories 36,
  120n106, 124, 125
Roman Catholic Church
  53, 55, 56, 57, 58n33,
  59, 64, 65, 68, 99
Roman civilization.......97
Roman law.......... 112n99
Roman political order
  ....108n91
Romanism 81
Romans...........74n52, 83
Romans 5:12, 18 ... 89n70
Rome ...42, 53, 54, 56, 90
Rousseau, Jean Jacques
  43n20, 89n71, 109n94
Rushdoony, R. J...35n12,
  87n68

S

sanctification 65
Schelling, Friedrich
  .... 70n51, 71n46
Schlegel, Friedrich 74n51,
  80n58, 89n70
science ... *xxvii, xxviii*, 29,
  30, 31, 33n9, 42, 44,
  47, 65, 72, 80n59, 100,
  104n86, 121, 122, 126
scientific investigation
 125
Scotland...................... 66
Scripture......... *xi*, 43n19,
  47n21, 60n24, 69n38,
  72n49, 79n56, 88n69,
  89n70, 92, 100,
  102n85, 113
secondary principles... 30

Semler, Johann Salomo
  .... 57n31
Siculus, Diodorus 84n64
slavery 39, 63, 66, 67n41,
  88, 118, 126
Socinus.......................64
Spain 40n17, 67
Spener 64
Spinoza, Baruch *xxviii*n4
spiritualism 77
St. Pierre, Bernardin
  .... 89n71
Statenvertaling ....*xi*,
  52n26, 78n55
stoicism 78
Stuarts 67n42
Switzerland 67

T

The Republic
  work of Plato ... 108n91
Thiers, Louis Adolphe
  ....93n76
Tholück, August ... 78n55,
  80n59
total depravity 65, 77n54
Turkish empire.......... 100
Two-Kingdom Theology
  .... 43n19
tyranny.......... *x, xxii*, 32,
  35n11, 67, 68n43,
  107n90

V

Van Alphen........... 74n52
van der Kemp............. 61
van der Palm, Johannes
  Henricus 70n44
Van Til, Cornelius..79n57
Vasa, Gustavus
  king of Sweden.. 75n52
Vatican 68n43

Von Haller, Albrecht
.... 104n86, 108n93,
110n95, 111n97
Von Kotzebue 90n71
von Muller, Johan 94n77
Von Savigny, Carl
Friedrich.......... 49n23,
73n50

W

Wesley, John 64

Whitefield, George 64
William of Orange 86n66
Wolff, Christian..... 57n31
Woods Jr., Thomas E.
...........................30n6
Wycliffe, John 64, 99

Z

Zwingli 64

www.ingramcontent.com/pod-product-compliance
Lightning Source LLC
Chambersburg PA
CBHW071513120626
46550CB00006B/2210